TASTE THE JOY OF EASTER

FR ANSELM GRÜN

Taste the Joy of Easter

Fifty movements for life

Translated by
Katherine Mistry-Tulloch & Andrew Tulloch

Original title: *Die Osterfreude auskosten*

Translated from the German

Translated by Katherine Mistry-Tulloch and Andrew Tulloch

ST PAULS Publishing
187 Battersea Bridge Road, London SW11 3AS, UK
www.stpauls.ie

ISBN 085439 630 6

ST PAULS, Alba House
2187 Victory Boulevard Staten Island, NY 10314, USA

ISBN 0-8189-0919-6

Distributed in Australia and New Zealand by
ST PAULS PUBLICATIONS
P O Box 906, Strathfield NSW 2135, Australia

Set by TuKan DTP, Fareham, Hampshire, UK
Printed by Interprint Ltd, Marsa, Malta

ST PAULS is an activity of the priests and brothers
of the Society of St Paul who proclaim the Gospel
through the media of social communication

Contents

Introduction

For the Early Church Eastertide constituted the middle of its year. For 50 days Christians would celebrate the Resurrection of the Lord. Enthralled, they would sing the Easter Hallelujah again and again. In singing they would express their joy at love's conquest of death, rejoicing in the fact that through the Resurrection we take part in the glory of Jesus Christ. Augustine, in one of his sermons, said about the Easter Hallelujah: "Let us sing the Hallelujah here on earth, where we are still in sorrow, so that one day we can sing it in heaven in safety… today let us sing, not in order to rejoice in the quiet, but in order to find consolation in distress. Sing as wanderers sing: Sing, but stride out! Singing, console yourself in distress, do not love misery! Sing and stride out!"

Many Christians today have lost a feeling for the mystery of Easter. They rejoice in the spring, but they associate the beautiful month of May less with Easter than with the experience of nature's return to life. The Early Church did not make this distinction: the Resurrection of Jesus Christ also renews creation. Easter was a Spring festival in its origins: the Passover Feast of the Jewish people replaced and reinterpreted the Canaanite Spring festival; the Christian faith has discerned that there lies within the mystery of Easter the true spring – life is stronger than death. The 'rigor mortis' of the tomb is transformed into a garden in bloom. The shackles that prevent us from living are struck off. Through the Resurrection we discover new life for the body and for the soul.

In the 50 days of Eastertide we follow the path of the Resurrection: it is a path that leads into ever-greater aliveness, freedom and joy. During this time we celebrate a path that leads us to become fully human, just as Christ became fully human in the incarnation. And in celebrating this path, we are able to get in touch, ever more closely, with the God-given potential that lies within us. When we walk along the way of the Resurrection, we walk free from all that stands in the way of true life, we stride out in order to experience the breadth and freedom of life; we awake from the sleep of our illusions and begin our journey towards true life. During Lent and Passiontide we meditated on the way of Jesus' suffering and so contemplated our own wounds. In Eastertide we now leave our injuries behind us, and turn to the life that seeks to blossom in our wounds. This is particularly helpful given the current tendency to dig up old wounds and root about in them: the path of Resurrection leads us into, and teaches us about, the life that is stronger than all injuries and inner obstructions.

The way of the Resurrection is a therapeutic way: it is an initiation into life. Normally therapy deals with our hurts and works on the repression and the inner wounds that mark our life story. There can be no doubt that this is useful work: but some stop at their injuries, and search endlessly for new methods of getting at old wounds. This kind of behaviour can easily lead to a situation where we end up going round in circles, dogged by an underlying depression – both of these phenomena are of course typical of the society in which we live. The way of the Resurrection is different: it starts with the life that is striving to blossom in us, with our abilities and our potential, with all that God wants to draw out of us. The Easter stories are just as therapeutic as the many healing stories recorded in the Gospels. The way of the Resurrection is open to us not only during Eastertide, but throughout the year. In situations where we feel the fragility of life, when depression and hopelessness overwhelm us, when disappointment and resignation spread, meditation on the way of the Resurrection can help us reconnect with the life that overcomes death, that rises from the tomb, that thaws the frozenness and the inner rigidity which keep us set in our ways, and leads us into the sheer breadth and freedom of the Resurrection. Every Sunday we celebrate the Resurrection of Jesus, which means that the way of the Resurrection is open to us Sunday after Sunday – giving us the opportunity to nurture the life within us, a life which during the week is all too often imprisoned by material constraints and eaten up by a deadly work rhythm. Spiritual exercises provide us with the same opportunity, where the way of the Resurrection can initiate us into the life that God has revealed to us in the Resurrection of Jesus, the life that God intends that we, too, should have.

In the meditations that follow I have selected an Easter Gospel for each week. Each day I have selected a figure or a symbol from the chosen Gospel and have attempted to show its relevance for our own lives. Thus each daily meditation provides an image that is meant to enable us to see and experience our lives with different eyes. Each image lets the mystery of the Resurrection appear in a different light. Having offered my interpretation I will then suggest exercises that are designed to help the life of the Resurrection flow into the reader's wounded psyche and to heal it. Alternatively, I will pose some questions, which we can only answer by the way we live.

I have supplemented the images and ideas in the Easter Gospels with 'archetypal' stories from the Acts of the Apostles. Luke is a master of narrative. His stories are like pictures in which we can see the light of the Resurrection shining in the lives of Jesus' disciples. Luke wrote the Acts of the Apostles as an Easter story; in it he describes the Apostles' way of the Resurrection. In their actions they experienced the Resurrection again and again. Luke wants to show us that we, too, can experience Resurrection in the various situations of our lives; that in us, too, prison walls can be broken down and we can stride out onto the 'new way' of life. For Luke, the Christian way is the 'new way', the way which guides us to true life. May this 'new way' become a way of the Resurrection for you, too – a way down which you can stride into the freedom and the joy of the Resurrection.

Celebrating the Resurrection

FIRST WEEK OF EASTER

• SUNDAY •

The women at the tomb

(Matthew 28:1)

In all the Easter Gospels it is the women who go to the tomb and meet the Risen One. Women were the first witnesses of the Resurrection. That must have been quite a challenge for the church of men. The scepticism felt by the men towards the reports of the women is shown in Luke's comment: "But these words seemed to them an idle tale, and they did not believe them." (Lk 24:11) Men need to see and grasp everything and are therefore not able to perceive the invisible. Women have a feeling for birth and death. They wait patiently beside the cross while the men flee. And so women become the witnesses of the new birth, of the new life that rises from the tomb.

In Matthew's Gospel the women "went to see the tomb" (Mt 28:1) at the break of the Sabbath, that is, after dusk set in. The word 'theorein' used in the Greek text means 'to see', 'to meditate on', 'to reflect on', 'to contemplate'. The women want to meditate at the tomb; they want to look mutely at the one who has touched their hearts. They obviously want to stand guard at the tomb. They want to be with Jesus even in his death, wait patiently by him and reflect on the mystery of his life. These women have the courage to go out into the night and to bear the grief that the tomb brings them. For this very reason they are able to experience the Resurrection and encounter the Risen One. Women are less afraid to visit the dying or to go to the cemetery and to sit by the graves of their relatives. Dying, for them, forms just as much part of life as does birth. Men prefer to give a wide berth to illness and death. Such subjects frighten them. They do not know what to say to someone who is dying, and they find it difficult to stand by those who are mourning. As a result, they are unable to experience the transformation of death. Women trust in life, even beyond death. Thus they spontaneously go towards the Risen One when they meet him on their way into the town: "And they came to him, took hold of his feet, and worshipped him" (Mt 28:9). They bow to the mystery of life that is stronger than death. They lovingly take hold of his feet. Because they are not afraid to 'get in touch with' the tomb, they are able to touch the Risen One and in him they touch and perceive the life that has conquered death. In Mark and Luke the women come to the tomb at the break of day in order to embalm Jesus' body with fragrant oils. They wish to perform this last labour of love. They prepared the fragrant ointments themselves from various spices. The love they had for Jesus did not end with his death, but extended to his dead body. At first glance, this care does not seem to make sense, because, given oriental weather conditions, the body could have started to decompose. But love always believes in a miracle. Love is stronger than death. The women have living proof of this: instead of finding the dead body of Jesus, they encounter the Risen One. Jesus is alive. Thus their love is not lost in the darkness of death, but it reaches the One who lives and who loves forever.

The Church today would be well advised to believe the women's message. Women have a healthy intuition for what awakens life within us. The Easter Gospels invite us to pay particular attention to what women have to tell us today: at home in the family, at work or in personal encounters. Can you find something in their words that is new and unusual? Can you sense in their words the quality of the Resurrection? Each of us, male and female, contains within us something of the feminine. The women who encountered the Risen One at the tomb encourage us to trust this 'anima' of ours – the soul, the interior premonitions of our heart. In the silent impulses of our heart we experience Resurrection. Here, frequently, the Risen One moves us and gives us the courage to get up, to approach a particular person, to say the word that is on the tip of our tongue, to tackle the problem which we are trying to evade. Today, therefore, listen consciously to the silent voices of your heart – voices that know that the Resurrection can become reality for you today, which trust in the life that conquers death and in the love that is stronger than death.

• MONDAY •

The angel of the Resurrection

(Matthew 28:2f)

All the Evangelists tell us that an angel appeared to the women at the tomb. The angel shows them the meaning of the emptiness. At first, they do not understand. The angel points them to the Risen One. He explains the words that Jesus said to them when he was alive. The presence and words of the shining angel enlighten the women, and they now understand the words of Jesus. Whenever Luke, in the Acts of the Apostles, narrates incidents in which an angel is at work, the Resurrection becomes reality for the apostles. We cannot talk about the Resurrection, then, without turning to the angel of the Resurrection. Where Resurrection happens, there the angel is, too. He shows us how surprising and incomprehensible events in our lives are in fact mysteries of the Resurrection.

Matthew seems to portray the angel as causing the Resurrection. As the day was dawning, the women went to see to the tomb, when an angel of the Lord descended from heaven and "came and rolled back the stone and sat on it. His appearance was like lightning, and his clothing white as snow" (Mt 28:2f). When an angel steps into our life, then we encounter Resurrection, our tomb is opened up and the stone that obstructs us is rolled away. Through the angel, God directly affects our own very concrete world. In the angel we experience God's light amid our darkness. Angels, according to theology, are created realities. In them the infinite and intangible God becomes tangible for us. An example of an angelic encounter such as this might be an experience of light amid our darkness. Suddenly there is a flash of light within us. The mist no longer envelops us. Suddenly everything becomes clear to us. We no longer feel soiled by the rubbish of everyday life against which we struggle ceaselessly. Our garments, like those of the angel, become white as snow. We become clean and pure and clear on the inside. The angel who does this might in actual fact be a person who talks to us or looks at us. In their gaze we recognise a light that in turn illuminates us. They radiate something, something which enlightens us and which puts us in touch with the light that dwells in our own soul. Every time we see this light in the eyes of a person, Resurrection happens for us.

In Mark, the stone had already been rolled away when the women came to the tomb. They entered the tomb and saw "a young man, dressed in a white robe, sitting on the right side; and they were alarmed" (Mk 16:5). In Luke, there are two men in shining garments who talk to the frightened women. In both of these Evangelists the reaction of the women is alarm or fright. "Angels are terrifying", says Rainer Maria Rilke. Through angels, another reality enters our life, the reality of God. And this reality is not only fascinating, but also always terrifying; a reality that can shake us to the core. There is nothing harmless or cute about angels. Resurrection is a mighty event. The tomb is broken open, and all that was rigid and set in death within now begins to move. The word 'phobeo' used in the Greek text of this Gospel story means not just 'to fear', 'to be frightened', 'to be startled', but also 'to put to flight', 'to flee'. Whoever is frightened by the angel of the Lord in this way cannot but move; they cannot just stay as they are, they cannot remain a spectator. Such a person feels the impact of the encounter in their heart and is forced to get up on their feet to confront the mighty truth of the angel.

In John's Gospel there are two angels sitting in the chamber of the tomb. Peter and John overlook the two angels in white garments. But Mary Magdalene recognises them as she enters the tomb chamber. The angels talk to her lovingly: "Woman, why are you weeping?" (Jn 20:13) The angels do not startle Mary Magdalene. They approach the mourning woman of their own accord. In their question one can sense understanding of her weeping. Through their question the two angels put something in motion. Mary of Magdala moves, she turns round and encounters the Risen One. When someone's words really move us, then without doubt Resurrection happens within us. If a person's words touch me in such a way as to make me turn round, turn about, the mystery of the Resurrection enters into my life. It need not necessarily be a person. The angel of the Resurrection can also talk to me through the word of God. If my heart receives the words of the Bible, and these words turn me round and turn me about, then I rise from the rigidity that held me tightly, then I experience Resurrection in myself.

Look out for the angel today, the angel who is with you in your tomb, in your darkness! Listen to the angel talking to you! Turn around when he enters into your life! Turn away from the many voices that would seem to suggest that there is nothing new under the sun! You, too, can experience the improbable, the unpredictable – the miracle of the Resurrection.

• TUESDAY •

The stone which blocks our access to life

(Matthew 28:2)

The stone which closes the tomb is a symbol of the inner obstacles that prevent us from living truly. Many of us have a real experience of these kinds of boulders, which obstruct our access to an authentic way of living – ballast from the past, the many hurts and wounds that stop us from simply getting up and going our way. Perhaps inhibitions paralyse us. Sometimes future events lie on our heart like stones. We are scared of a meeting, of an exam, of a difficult operation. Sometimes there are people that weigh on us like a boulder. They have power over us. We are unable to breathe when they are near. They cramp us. They block us. In their presence we do not show ourselves as we truly are. We are scared of their loudness and blustering, of the destructive power that emanates from them. Like a stone they block our access to the life that is striving to blossom in us.

When Resurrection happens, an angel comes down from heaven and rolls the stone aside. The weight that stops us from living is removed. We can breathe freely again. Suddenly we no longer feel the stone's weight. The angel seats itself on the boulder like a victor. The boulder becomes a symbol of the victory of life over death. It reminds us that a miracle has happened to us, that our tomb has been broken open and that we are now able to get up onto our feet. We might have reflected and attempted in many conversations to free ourselves from the weight of the boulder. But our attempts served no purpose. Then, suddenly an angel enters our life, and without knowing what is happening to us, we feel the boulder being rolled aside, and life enters once again.

Some have a hardened heart. They have so cut themselves off from their feelings that their heart has become stone. They are cold, excluded from life. Behind the boulder that closes the tomb the dead body is decomposing. In the story of Lazarus the stone that covers the entrance to the tomb of Jesus' friend is a symbol of his 'non-relatedless', his lack of relation to others. Those who lie behind a boulder are no longer in relation to other people. And when the human person is deprived of relatedness, they rot, "there is a stench" (Jn 11:39). The love of Jesus reaches beyond the stone. It is strong enough to re-establish relations with Lazarus across the stone. It reaches right into the tomb. Jesus shows his love by weeping and by being greatly disturbed (Jn 11:35.38). The people watching sense his love: "See how he loved him!" (Jn 11:36) But Jesus does not stop at the feeling of love. "Take away the stone" (Jn 11:39), he commands. Then he looks up to heaven, to his Father, and calls out in a loud voice, "Lazarus, come out!" (Jn 11:43) The voice of Jesus cannot penetrate through stone. But when the stone is taken away, the word of Jesus reaches us even when we have already died, even if much in us has already decomposed. Jesus' friendship with Lazarus is strong enough to bring the dead man back to life. The word of love calls the dead man out of the tomb and liberates him from all his bindings. Jesus, through his word, wants to liberate us too: from the shackles of fear and of conformism, from all our bindings and the 'sudarium' behind which we hide our true face. The word of love empowers us to step out of the tomb and remove all that masks our true face.

In the story of Lazarus the love of Jesus reaches into the dead heart of Lazarus and awakes it to new life. In the Resurrection of Jesus the love of the Father sends the angel to roll aside the boulder. The love of the Father reaches right into the darkness of death, the rigor mortis, the decomposition. The love of the Father awakens the Son. And the Father will do the same for us. When we have imprisoned ourselves in the tomb of our fear and rigidity, the Father will send us an angel, too. The Father's love will roll aside the stone that traps us in the tomb, and reawaken us to new life.

Which 'stone' is obstructing your life? Name it and try to hold it out to God in prayer. You could, if you wish, pick up some stones from the ground and on them, write down what it is that weighs on you and what it is that stops you from living. Then throw the stones into a stream or a lake. Celebrate the Resurrection by throwing as many stones as you wish, and hurl them with all your might. Imagine that with each stone one more blockage within you disappears. After this, try to breathe freely, to feel the breadth within that comes once the stones no longer stand in the way of your living.

• WEDNESDAY •

The guardians of death

(Matthew 28:4)

In Matthew's story of the Resurrection, Roman soldiers guard the tomb of Jesus. The High Priests and Pharisees are afraid that Jesus' words concerning of his Resurrection might become true, and so they seek to take precautions and ask Pilate to have the tomb guarded: "Pilate said to them, 'You have a guard of soldiers; go, make it as secure as you can.' So they went with the guard and made the tomb secure by sealing the stone." (Mt 27:65f) But when the angel of the Lord comes down from heaven and rolls aside the stone, "for fear of him the guards shook and became like dead men." (Mt 28:4) There can be no safeguard against God. You can seal and guard the tomb as much as you like. When God intercedes in our life, the guardians of death fall to the ground. God cannot be locked into a tomb.

The guards who keep watch over the One who died to ensure he does not return to life, drop down as if dead, while the One who died rises to life. This is the paradox of the Resurrection. Such guardians of death exist within our own selves. They make sure that everything stays the same, that our own cherished beliefs are not shaken. These guards keep watch over our principles – whatever we have got in our heads, must surely be right. This is what the Pharisees thought. But they reckoned without God. They are obviously scared that their own ideas might not correspond to reality after all, and so they seek to impose these ideas with force. They need soldiers to consolidate their power. Fear always results in guards being posted and soldiers being ordered to fight.

We, too, have this fear inside us. We are often afraid of life simply as it is. We want to press life into moulds that suit us. We are frightened of God, frightened that he might act in a way that goes entirely against what we desire. So we place guards in front of the cherished beliefs that govern our religious life too. Our beliefs must not be shaken, and we safeguard ourselves against God. But the God of the Resurrection rejects all our beliefs. When God breaks into our life, the result is an earthquake; the guardians of death drop to the ground.

These guardians of death are not only found within, however. There are plenty of them in the world around us. There will always be those who want to cement their power, who want to impose it, at any cost. The Pharisees made use of a lie in order to stay in power. When the guards were unable to prevent the Resurrection of Jesus, they had to be bribed by the High Priests so they would not communicate the truth. They were asked to spread false rumours, so that the power of the High Priests and their own convictions might not be shaken. There are many tyrants who twist the truth and who have the tomb of their people guarded so that no prophet will stand up and question their power. The guardians of the tomb stand for the political dimension of the Resurrection. Even if political parties, tyrants, power-hungry leaders guard their country's tomb with the utmost care, they will not succeed. God's power is stronger. It will resurrect life. It will come like an earthquake, breaking down the blocks of earthly power that the powerful had thought were cemented so firmly together, and will leave no stone unturned. Then the guardians of death stand no chance. They cannot prevent the victory of life, the resurrection of truth. In what areas of your life do you have guardians of death? Why do you try to keep the lid tight down on certain thoughts? Why do you hide behind norms and principles? Hold your guardians of death up to the light of the angel of the Resurrection! The angel of the Resurrection will throw them to the ground, so that you may rise.

• THURSDAY •

The tomb of fear and resignation

(Acts 3)

The Resurrection, the 'Rising from the Dead' necessarily involves a 'rising'. Many prefer to remain lying in the tomb of their fear and resignation, of their disappointments and hurts. They have settled in the tomb because they are frightened of living. Rising always entails exposing oneself to hurt. When I rise I have to face life. But many are frightened of doing this. And so they prefer to remain lying down. The Greek word for 'to rise', 'egeiren', is used to describe both the

Resurrection of Jesus and his commands to the sick to get up and walk in the many narratives of healing. In these narratives of healing there is Resurrection, too. People get the courage to free themselves from the shackles of their fear, to break the inhibitions and inner blockages which bound them to their beds, so that they get up, take their bed under their arm and walk about (cf. Jn 5:1-10). Luke reports not only the stories of the healings of Jesus, but also those performed by the Apostles. In these healings the mystery of the Resurrection is continued in the Disciples. Luke wants to show us that the Resurrection was not a unique event, that through our belief in the Resurrection of Jesus we may ourselves experience Resurrection and awaken others to life.

In Acts 3 Luke tells how Peter and John go to the Temple to pray around the ninth hour, that is, the hour of Jesus' death. "And a man lame from birth was being carried in." (Acts 3:2) When the man begs the Apostles for alms, Peter says to him: "'I have no silver or gold, but what I have I give you; in the name of Jesus Christ of Nazareth, stand up and walk.' And he took him by the right hand and raised him up; and immediately his feet and ankles were made strong. Jumping up, he stood and began to walk." (Acts 3:6-8) Through Jesus' power the Disciples are able to raise the man who had been paralysed from birth. The riches which the Disciples give is the faith in the Risen One. And this faith has the power to lead others to Resurrection. It encourages them to let go of their inhibitions and to trust in the strength which God has given them. In the paralysed man this faith finds expression in his leaping around the temple and praising of God. A large crowd gathers. And now there is Resurrection in Peter, too. He has the courage to speak to all people. This uneducated man announces to the people the Good News of the Resurrection: "You killed the Author of life, whom God raised from the dead. To this we are witnesses." (Acts 3:15) Jesus is the author of life. Who believes in him, finds in him true life. Peter concludes his sermon with the words: "When God raised up his servant, he sent him first to you, to bless you by turning each of you from your wicked ways." (Acts 3:26) The aim of the Resurrection of Jesus is that the people are blessed through him and embark on a new path, the path of life, instead of the old path of wickedness.

Yet the experience of the Resurrection goes even further. Peter and John are arrested by the temple guards and thrown into prison. The next day they are questioned. Peter is without fear. We can tell from his words that he is full of joy at the Resurrection: Resurrection which he was able to experience not only in Jesus, but also in the paralysed man and in himself. He is not intimidated by the Sadducees. They can sense the frankness in his words, the interior freedom which the healing that was carried out in the name of the crucified and risen Lord has given him. The leaders of the people want to ban him from preaching sermons. But Peter replies in the same spirit of freedom which filled him when he spoke of the Resurrection of Jesus: "Whether it is right in God's sight to listen to you rather than to God, you must judge; for we cannot keep from speaking about what we have seen and heard." (Acts

4:19f) The experience of the Resurrection cannot be banned by threats.

Trust the power of the Resurrection! Shake off your paralysis and inhibitions! Stand up and go your way, do not fear what people might think of you! When you are frightened of a task, repeat to yourself the word of Jesus: "Stand up, take your bed and walk!" Take your fear under your arm, and confront the problem! Take it in hand! Then you will experience the Resurrection. You, too, can get up and walk. The power of the Resurrection is in you. No effort to rise is needed. You have only to trust the Resurrection, the Resurrection which Christ wants you, too, to experience.

• FRIDAY •

Awakened to reality

(Acts 2:23f)

The New Testament's favourite word for the Resurrection is the Greek word 'egeiren' or 'egerte'. It means 'to awaken', 'to arouse from sleep', but also 'to rise', 'to raise up'. Greek has another word for Resurrection, 'anastasis'. This describes more the active raising up, whereas 'egeiren' is more passive, placing God's action at the centre: it is God the Father who raises Jesus from the dead. In the sermons of the Acts of the Apostles Peter and Paul again and again point out that God did not "hand Jesus over to corruption", but that he resurrected him from the dead: "this man, handed over to you according to the definite plan and foreknowledge of God, you crucified and killed by the hands of those outside the law. But God raised him up, having freed him from death, because it was impossible for him to be held in its power." (Acts 2:23f) In the Resurrection, God acts on his Son Jesus Christ. Because God stands by his Son he sets him free from the power of death. Because Jesus is in God's hand even in death, the merciful hand of the Father loosed the pangs of death.

God, who awakened Jesus from death, will awaken us too. We, too, are in God's hand, in life and in death. Jesus, the good shepherd, promises us that no one can pluck us out of his Father's hand (Jn 10:29). Death no longer has ultimate power over us. The hand of the Father is stronger. And yet Jesus died, and we too will die. But death is not final. God will awaken us from the sleep of death, so that we will rise with Christ to eternal life. We will not rise through any power of our own, but because the Father resurrects us, because God himself will act lovingly upon us.

But this awakening does not just refer to the death that comes at the end of our life. Even now, we keep drifting into the sleep of death. Many people live as if in a slumber. They live in a world full of illusions. They deceive themselves. They are not in touch with reality. The Indian Jesuit Anthony de Mello said that mysticism is an awakening to reality. Whoever experiences God, wakes up. Mysticism is not just concerned with the enlightened, who are completely penetrated by God's light, but with those who have been woken up, who have awakened, with people who through their spiritual path have become free of the illusions they had created regarding themselves and their life. Because they encountered God, they woke up. God himself has woken them, roused them. Sometimes this process of waking up can be painful. In the morning, we often resist waking up and getting out of bed. It would be so much nicer to keep dozing and to continue living in the images our dreams have spun.

Romano Guardini says that in his youth he lived as if in bed, with his bedclothes drawn over his head, in a world of his own without any reference to reality. It was only during his university studies that he woke up and confronted reality. There are many people who go through phases when they do not really live, when they move about in a dream world, in an unreal world without any reference to the real one. Belief in the awakening of Jesus means that we ask God to wake us up from our slumber, to open our eyes so that we may see the truth. There are many different kinds of sleep from which God rouses us. There is the sleep of security. We cradle ourselves in security. We deceive ourselves and do not see that it is God's hand that holds us and not our own. Then there is the sleep which is a flight from reality. There are people who fall asleep whenever things get uncomfortable or unpleasant. They are constantly tired and flee into sleep. They cannot bear reality. I heard a story about a teacher who had to give up her job because she simply could not get out of bed in the morning. Not hearing the alarm clock was obviously a subconscious attempt to escape from the harsh reality, a subconscious resistance to what life demanded of her.

Try to go through this day fully awake! Watch yourself: in what areas of your life do you escape into illusions, do you withdraw into sleep? Open your eyes! Look at reality the way it is! Wake up and get up! Live attentively, raised, resurrected!

• SATURDAY •

Resurrection as liberation

(Acts 16)

Matthew describes the Resurrection as a great earthquake (Mt 28:2). In the Resurrection of Jesus something gets moving. The foundations of our life are shaken. In the Acts of the Apostles Luke tells how in our lives, too, the Resurrection can manifest itself as an earthquake. Paul and Silas are thrown into the inner prison and their feet are fastened in stocks: "About midnight Paul and Silas were praying and singing hymns to God, and the prisoners were listening to them. Suddenly there was an earthquake, so violent that the foundations of the prison were shaken; and immediately all the doors were opened and everyone's chains were unfastened." (Acts 16:25f) This is a beautiful image of what it is to experience Resurrection. All too often we feel like we are in prison, in the prison of our fear, our loneliness, our depression. Sometimes the patterns of our life story constitute a prison from which we cannot break free: we are prisoners of our perfectionism, of our compulsion to blame ourselves when things go wrong, of our narcissism, of our neurotic and constant projection of an idealised image of ourselves to the outside world. When we praise God from our prison, in the confidence that in spite of all our fetters we are in God's good hand, then we, too, can experience the earth moving, as Paul and Silas did. Then the walls which are keeping us prisoner begin to shake. Then doors are opened. We get in touch with ourselves. We no longer live outside of ourselves, but we gain access to our heart. The doors that connect us to others are flung open: suddenly they can come in, and we have access to them. We are able, then, to encounter others in a real way. The fetters drop off, the fetters of our fear, of our inhibitions and our paralysis. We feel free. The mighty earthquake rouses the jailer. When he sees the door of the prison open, the jailer draws his sword and is about to kill himself, but Paul reassures him, saying that he should not harm himself, as the prisoners have not escaped. Then the jailer drops to his feet trembling, and asks, "'Sirs, what must I do to be saved?' They answered, 'Believe on the Lord Jesus, and you will be saved, you and your household.'" (Acts 16:30f) Here the jailer could be taken as an internal image representing our old patterns, our perfectionism, our ambition, our distrust, our yearning for security. Some respond to the liberation from their fetters with euphoria. They think that everything has changed. Now they can throw all inhibiting life patterns overboard. Now, they think, they are completely free and their past no longer has a hold over them. In their enthusiasm, they throw the baby out with the bath water. We should not and cannot simply destroy our patterns. If we tried to do so we would feel their absence sorely. What we should do is get in touch with them. When, believing in Christ, we encounter them, they no longer have a hold over us: they will be at our service, like the jailer, who takes Paul and Silas into his home, washes their wounds and is baptised: "He brought them up into the house and set food before them; and he and his entire household rejoiced that he had become a believer in God." (Acts 16:34) We cannot simply leave aside the experiences that have marked our life story. When we reconcile ourselves with them, they will heal our wounds and nourish us. We become the guests at a joyful banquet, and everything in us comes alive. Then the patterns no longer take the role of a jailer, but that of a baptised brother. They have been transformed. Our ambition no longer holds us prisoner, but it becomes a source of life; our perfectionism is liberated from its compulsiveness, and now serves its real purpose of helping us deal attentively with things.

In the Acts of the Apostles Luke has transposed the Resurrection of Jesus into the concrete situations in which the Disciples of Jesus found themselves. He wants to show us a way to break out of our inner prison: the way of prayer, of praising God in the middle of the night of our life. Today, try to praise God without any ulterior motive: perhaps you will see the prison walls come tumbling down, your fetters dropping off and the doors connecting you with other people flying open. When you want nothing from God, when you praise him simply because he is God, you will receive an inner taste of freedom amid the prison of your night, of the Resurrection amid your compulsions, of trust amid your fears.

Encounter with the Risen One

SECOND WEEK OF EASTER

• SUNDAY •

Seeing the Risen One in the midst of our everyday lives

(Matthew 28:7)

In the Gospels of Mark and Matthew the angel urges the women to tell the Disciples, "He has been raised from the dead, and indeed he is going ahead of you to Galilee; there you will see him." (Mt 28:7) The Disciples, says the angel, should return to Galilee. They will not encounter Jesus in the holy city of Jerusalem, but at the place where they live and work, in the midst of their everyday lives. Galilee was the country where Jews and Gentiles lived together. Galilee therefore stands not only for everyday life, but also for the 'mixture of different peoples', the mixture which is our own lives. Our life is Galilee. In our own very selves Jews and Gentiles live together alongside each other. In us is closeness to God and distance from God, belief and unbelief, love and hatred, aliveness and rigidity, light and darkness – all alongside each other. And in our everyday lives, too, we live shoulder to shoulder with people who look for God and people who aren't really bothered about him, with people we love and with those with whom we struggle.

In the midst of this mixture of our Galilee we will see the Risen One. This is the angel's promise. The angel appeals to our eyes and the sense of sight. With our eyes we will see the Risen One: initially it is not about hearing, but about seeing. We need new eyes to recognise the Risen One in the midst of our lives. When we look at someone's face and see pain giving way to joy, hope and confidence – then we behold the Risen One. We see him, too, when we observe conflicts resolving, tensions dissolving in the course of a conversation, people becoming reconciled with each other. Resurrection is therefore something to be seen even though it is described by the Evangelists as something invisible, something that cannot be observed. We can see Resurrection if we watch nature blossoming everywhere in the spring with eyes that can see. Not for nothing does many an Easter song follow its description of the Resurrection with a description of the blossoming of creation. J. M. C. Crum wrote: "Now the green blade riseth from the buried grain / Wheat that in the dark earth many days has lain; / Love lives again, that with the dead has been; / Love is come again like wheat that springeth green." In the blossom which opens, in the grass which turns green, in the colourful meadows of spring we behold the Risen One; and life shows itself to be stronger than death. Spring is also associated with love. May is the month of love. When nature blossoms, when during the mating season the birds pair and sing their most beautiful songs, then in people, too, there blossoms the yearning for a love that enchants everything.

Look carefully today at nature sprouting around you and recognise the power of the Resurrection in it! Take note of the love that blossoms in your own life! The Risen One has gone before you – he is already in your life, in your Galilee. All you need are eyes that see, to discover the Risen One right in the midst of the 'mixture' which is your life. When you see him, your Galilee becomes transformed, and Resurrection happens in the very midst of your life.

• MONDAY •

Turning to life

(Luke 24:5f)

Returning to the tomb, the women in Luke's Gospel meet two men in shining garments who ask them a challenging question: "Why do you look for the living among the dead? He is not here, but has risen." (Lk 24:5) The two heavenly creatures here give the women a kind of proverb. In Chapter 24 of his Gospel Luke describes how the Easter faith of the Disciples grows gradually – and in doing so shows how our own faith in the Resurrection may grow. Like the women we, too, probably start by looking for the Risen One where we last saw him, in his tomb. While the women go to the tomb, to the place of terror, the Emmaus disciples turn away. They initially flee from the place of their disappointment. But then both the Emmaus disciples and the women turn around and meet in Jerusalem. While they are still talking, the Risen One appears to them in bodily form. He eats with them and talks to them; he leads them to near Bethany and is raised into heaven before their very eyes. Only now do the Disciples truly believe. And now they sing the praises of God with great joy.

Luke describes the growth of the Easter faith with great sensitivity. The story begins with a search for the dead body; this is understandable, but it does not lead to an experience of the Risen One. We ourselves often look for life among the dead; we seek for life in the dead letter of the law and think that the essence of life lies in the obeying of all commands, that we must do everything right. I know a woman who since her childhood has been asking one question: "Am I doing it right? Is it right like this?" But the quest to do everything right, always, cannot lead her to life, she is looking for the Living One among the dead. Others search for life in money and possessions: but they are dead things. Jesus tells the young man who wants to follow him, "Let the dead bury their own dead; but as for you, go and proclaim the kingdom of God." (Lk 9:60) Money, possessions, power, status – they are all dead things. We should bury them and leave them dead and buried and turn to life, to the Kingdom of God. Life does not become true life until God is part of it: when God reigns, when it is filled with God's light and love.

Dead also is the young man of Luke's parable in chapter 15 of his Gospel: the young man who squanders his inheritance and leads a dissolute life, who quells his hunger with pods, with cheap stuff that does not truly nourish. External pleasures, living a dissipated life, letting oneself go, being governed by one's whims: these things are, for Luke, dead. We cannot find life in them. Only when the son turns back and returns to the house where he is truly at home, does he become alive again. The father calls for a feast to be prepared, a feast of life, “for this son of mine was dead and is alive again; he was lost and is found!” (Lk 15:24) Life cannot be found in death’s dominion. The two heavenly messengers show the women the way to find the Living One. They refer to the words of Jesus: “Remember how he told you, while he was still in Galilee, that the Son of Man must be handed over to sinners, and be crucified, and on the third day rise again.” (Lk 24:6f) Because they remember Jesus’ words, the women are able to believe in the Resurrection. In the words of Jesus they find life. When they remember his words or when they, as the Latin word ‘recordamini’ puts it, ponder the words in their heart, when – translating the word literally – they ‘bring them back into the heart’, then the mystery of the Resurrection becomes clear to them.

In what areas of your life do you look for the Living One among the dead? What should you bury because it has long been dead? You may remember past conflicts, hurts which still pain you, disappointments that cause you bitterness. All that is dead within you, write it down on a piece of paper and bury it in the garden or in a flowerpot. Sow flower seeds on it, so that new life can bloom on the final resting place of your hurts. The flowers are to remind you to leave your wounded life story alone, to stop digging up the soil of its final resting place. Otherwise nothing will ever be able to bloom on it.

• TUESDAY •

The Risen One on the road with us

(Luke 24:13ff)

The most beautiful Easter story is told by Luke: he describes how two disciples turn away from Jerusalem disappointed; they leave the place of their disappointment; they want nothing further to do with their past. But they are still talking to each other; they discuss what has happened. In conversation they seek to explore why everything happened as it did and what significance it might have for them. Because they do not simply cease communication altogether and because they do not close their eyes to what has happened, Jesus is able to intervene in their conversation and guide it in another direction. But Jesus does not have an easy time of it. Luke describes the state of these disciples. They are not blind, but nevertheless their eyes are unable to see Jesus truly, and they do not recognise him. The pair do not believe the women who tell them about the angel's apparition. Jesus accuses them of not understanding and of being slow of heart. Because they are without understanding, they do not understand what happened in Jerusalem. When Jesus accuses them of being slow at heart he probably means that their hearts are 'uncreative', that they themselves cannot envisage other solutions than those they are used to. They are dull and do not understand what is new and unusual about the Resurrection.

As the first step in his transformation of these

slow and thick-witted Disciples Jesus lets them talk. He challenges them to present their view of all that has passed. The two begin by accusing him, asking him whether he was the only guest in Jerusalem during the Passover who had not heard about what had happened. The crucifixion of Jesus, they say, is the talk of the town. And then they present their view of things as they see them. They had placed all their hopes in Jesus. He was a prophet, mighty in deed and word. They hoped that he would set Israel free. But now it is the third day after his death. On the third day the soul separates from the body, and there is therefore no longer any hope that he might be rescued from the throes of death. Jesus lets them relate all they have experienced and their view of things, but then he begins to talk. He takes their information and their feelings seriously; at the same time he confronts them with the words from the Scriptures. Using the Scriptures he is able to show the disciples a different way of looking at things. Jesus interprets his own destiny as being in accordance with the Scriptures: although it was necessary for Jesus to suffer, the suffering was only the transition to his Resurrection. The disciples listen, initially unbelieving. But the words of Jesus go straight to their hearts, and they ask him to stay with them.

This story presents us with an important motif in Luke's narrative of the Resurrection: the Risen One walks with us on our path. When we are on the path, when we do not simply stop and give up, then the Risen One is by our side. And we can talk to him, we can tell him about everything that we do not understand in our lives: using the

Scriptures he will interpret our lives for us and show us a new way of looking at them. The Risen One allows us to ask him to stay with us when it turns evening, when the darkness falls within and around us. He goes with us into the places where we stop, in order to be with us. This would appear to be the consoling message of this tale: "So he went in to stay with them" (Lk 24:29).

Imagine that the Risen One will walk with you today along the paths you take, that he is by your side when you go to work, that he accompanies you when you go for a walk, that he is by your side wherever you may be! When you do not understand your life, ask him what it all means! Hold your disappointments out to him! Perhaps then you will discover for yourself a deeper meaning behind all that is happening to you and around you.

• WEDNESDAY •

Was it not necessary that this should happen to me...?

(Luke 24:26)

What the Emmaus disciples have to say about Jesus' fate in Jerusalem could be understood as an image of our own inner reality. The words of the disciples would probably sound as follows in our mouths: "We were hoping that our lives would be successful, that we would be mighty in word and deed, that we would achieve much, that we would make it in some way. But all our plans have been crossed. We have failed. Everything has broken down within us. Everything is without hope. There is no point to it all." Jesus does not reproach us for thinking thus, but tries to interpret what has happened in a different way, according to the Scriptures. The key to his new perspective is: "Was it not necessary that the Messiah should suffer these things and then enter into his glory?" (Lk 24:26) Translated into our own situation, this sentence would read: "Was it not necessary that this should happen to you, so that all would turn out well with you? Did not all that happened to you, happen so that you could be freed from the illusions that you have created yourself about your life, so that you grow into the true image of yourself, as God intended?"

For ten years I would go walking through the Steigerwald forest for a week in the company of some young people. On these walks I would often give the following sentence as a meditation for the silent periods: "Was it not necessary that the Messiah should suffer these things and then enter into his glory?" We would walk in silence for an hour. During this hour the young people were asked to repeat this sentence to themselves again and again and to contemplate their whole life in the light of these words. When I allow this word to work on my disappointments, on the hurts I received during childhood, on the wounds from my time as a boarder and at school, on the misunderstandings within the monastery, on the frustrations at work, then I stop complaining about them. I can see my life story with fresh eyes. Everything is allowed to be as it is, everything is good. Everything has served to help me grow into the true image of myself, as God intended. Through all the experiences of my life God has moulded me and formed me (even me) in the way he intended from the beginning. For me these words of Jesus have assumed the utmost importance in helping me to reconcile myself to my life story. I often give them to people to meditate on. The words help them see their life with fresh eyes, and suddenly they discover a meaning within the meaninglessness, hope amid the disappointment, trust amid the distrust.

Jesus' way of showing understanding to the disciples provides a good example to follow in our pastoral work, whatever form that may take. We should allow people to tell us what they have experienced, what they are suffering from, what has disappointed them. We should not seek to soothe away their trouble but rather let it stand as it is, in the way it is told us. What we can do, however, is to confront their life story with the Scriptures and interpret it in the light of the Scriptures, in order to help them understand it better. For ourselves, too, these crucial words of Jesus to his Disciples should be of great help. Ask yourself today whether, in all that you experience, your perspective is really the only one possible! And let Jesus' words work on all the thoughts that occur to you today: "Was it not necessary that this should happen to you, so that it would be well with you? Was it not necessary that you should go through this suffering in order to liberate you from your illusions? Was it not necessary that you should suffer at your own hands, so that you would embark on the road of transformation, so that you would come into the glory that God has intended for you? Do you believe that God has led you in everything, that he has carried you in his hand? What does God want to tell you through all you have experienced? What destination do you think God might have in mind for you, given all the experiences he has led you through? Against the backdrop of your life story, can you discern your own personal vocation, your mission?"

• THURSDAY •

Breaking the bread

(Luke 24:30f)

Jesus goes with the disciples "to stay with them" (Lk 24:29). That, according to Luke, is the meaning of the Resurrection: Jesus walks with us down all the paths we take and he shares our meal with us wherever we stay. For Luke the Eucharist in particular is the place where we encounter the Risen One. His description of it is striking: "When he was at the table with them, he took bread, blessed and broke it, and gave it to them. Then their eyes were opened, and they recognised him; and he vanished from their sight." (Lk 24:30f) Jesus is the disciples' guest. And yet he acts as the paterfamilias when he himself takes the bread, says grace, breaks the bread and shares it out. By the way in which Jesus does this the disciples obviously recognise the

Risen One, and henceforth the daily breaking of the bread is the place where they know the Risen One to be among them. In the breaking of the bread, in each Eucharist, it is the risen Jesus himself who breaks the bread for the Disciples and who shows them his love. And the Disciples respond always to the presence of Jesus with joy: "Day by day, as they spent much time together in the temple, they broke bread at home and ate their food with glad and generous hearts" (Acts 2:46).

No other Evangelist tells us of so many meals as Luke does. Time after time Jesus is shown sharing a meal with the Disciples, the Pharisees, the sinners and tax collectors. The Eucharist is for Luke a continuation of the many meals that Jesus shared with the people and in which he made visible to them God's goodness and love of humankind. In the Eucharist Christ himself comes among us again. He talks to us and helps us to understand our lives. We are able to experience communion with him and to rejoice in it. But we do not see him. Luke describes the disappearance of Jesus with a typical Greek expression: "he vanished from their sight" (Lk 24:31). God appears to us and at the same time he vanishes from our sight. The disciples begin to see the light. In the man who breaks the bread for them they recognise Jesus himself, and at the same time they no longer see him. They see him with their inner eyes. If in the Eucharist we look with these inner eyes, then we will see the Risen One himself present among us: in the meal that we share, in the bread that we break for each other. If you have an opportunity today to take part in the Eucharistic Feast, then imagine that

Jesus, the Risen One himself is present. He himself breaks the bread. He speaks words of love to you. Open your heart to these words, so that it may begin to burn in the same way as the hearts of the Emmaus disciples did. And when the priest places the broken bread on your hand during communion, imagine that it is handed to you by the Risen One, given to you to heal and reconnect all that is broken and divided, to pick up the broken pieces of your life story and shape them into a living chain. May your eyes be opened and may you recognise Jesus himself, who gives himself to you in the sign of the bread, in order to share his life with you and to make your heart burn through his love.

• FRIDAY •

Sharing our faith in an Easter community

(Luke 24:34f)

Because Jesus set the hearts of the Emmaus disciples alight, they leave at that very hour in order to return to Jerusalem. They feel compelled to tell their friends about what they have heard and seen; they cannot keep their enthusiasm to themselves. When the pair arrives in Jerusalem late at night, they find the Eleven and the other disciples assembled. "They were saying, 'The Lord has risen indeed, and he has appeared to Simon!'

Then they told what had happened on the road, and how he had been made known to them in the breaking of the bread." (Lk 24:34f) Those who stayed at home and those who have returned from abroad tell each other what they have experienced. And their tales become a confession: "The Lord has risen indeed." The experience is captured in two words: "He was seen and he was recognised." Simon saw the Risen One, and the Emmaus disciples recognised him when he broke the bread. Seeing alone is not enough, we have also to understand what we see: if we do so, then Resurrection will happen for us, too. As the Disciples are telling each other what they have experienced, the Risen One himself comes amongst them and gives them the sign of peace.

The way in which the Disciples share their faith provides us with a beautiful image of the Church. The Church is a community of people who share what they have experienced, what they have seen and come to realise. Some share what they have experienced themselves, others refer to the experience of a third party, as in the case of the disciples in Jerusalem who tell of the appearance of the Risen One to Simon. Each one of us has a tale to tell about our journey on the road. When our experience on the road has opened our eyes and made our hearts burn within us, then we have encountered the Risen One. For Luke, whenever our heart is moved in its innermost core or, as Paul Tillich puts it, whenever something "speaks to us unconditionally", there, infallibly, we experience the Resurrection. They are everyday experiences: conversations, encounters, meals, breaking of bread, walks, communal outings. We talk much to each other and keep meeting new people, but often the conversation remains mere talk and the meeting mere contact. Where there is true dialogue, where eyes are opened, where our hearts start to burn as we talk – there is truly Resurrection, there we meet the Risen One himself, who appears to us in the shape of a companion on the road.

Today some put their experience of God all too much on display. It makes one think of spiritual prostitution. The Disciples share their experience with each other in a different way: the words they use are very restrained; they talk about what has happened. And what has happened is quite matter-of-fact. They interpret all that has happened to them through their faith, because in their experiences they have recognised Christ himself. They do not force their experiences upon each other, but confess that the Lord has truly risen. They stand by their experiences. Because of this approach others are able to share in their experiences. In this way a true community of believers, of people who have experienced God, comes into existence. When people talk honestly but also carefully and attentively about what they have experienced on their path and how they have interpreted and understood it for themselves, then suddenly the Risen One himself comes and stands among them, and the conversation becomes an experience of Resurrection. A kind of 'density' is created, in which we touch the essential, in which God's presence appears tangible. Augustine tells of a conversation with his mother Monica where all of a sudden, time stood still and the pair touched God. Luke stands in the tradition of the great Greek narrators, he tells his stories in such a way that our eyes are opened and our hearts are warmed.

What would you like to tell the people who have become dear to you? Have you often pondered in your heart what you would like to say to your friend, and have you always held it back? To live the Resurrection would mean that now you stand by the inner impulse that urges you to open yourself to the other person. When you dare to say what has been forming in your heart for a long time, you will learn how a new relationship is created, how hearts begin to burn, how the Risen One himself talks within you.

• SATURDAY •

Doubt and faith

(Luke 24:36-49)

In Luke's Gospel Easter Day concludes with the appearance of Jesus to all the Disciples. The Disciples have just told each other what they had experienced, and they have confessed to each other that the Lord has truly risen. Now that the Risen One incarnate is among them, they are startled and frightened. They think that they are seeing a phantasm, something merely in the imagination. The Disciples are obviously still struggling to believe in the Resurrection. Jesus attempts to ease their doubts in three steps. First of all, he talks to them.

He is no figment of the imagination. He really is there. He talks to them just as he did when he was alive. But Jesus knows clearly what the Disciples are thinking and he senses that a second step is required to remove their doubts about his identity. So he invites them: "Look at my hands and my feet; see that it is I myself. Touch me and see; for a ghost does not have flesh and bones as you see that I have." (Lk 24:39) Then he shows them his hand and feet and the Disciples realise that the Risen One and the master whom they have followed are one and the same. Jesus is not a mere apparition. He is risen in body and soul. In his narrative Luke contradicts the idea that Jesus possessed an 'illusory' body, an idea which was obviously popular in the Early Church. The Evangelist seeks to tell Christians that Jesus has truly risen, that his Resurrection is not just something that went on in the heads of the Disciples: he has become visible, tangible, touchable.

The Disciples react to Jesus' words and to the touching of his hands and feet with surprise and joy. They are overwhelmed by joy. They are rendered utterly speechless by joy. It is a joy which still lacks faith, a joy which exists only in feeling. The joy is enthusiasm, but it cannot be sustained. It is a joy which is filled with wonder but which does not touch faith in itself. Faith always involves recognition and confession. To enable the Disciples to progress from a mere feeling of joy to faith, Jesus says to them, "Have you anything here to eat?" (Lk 24:41) They give him a piece of fried fish, "and he took it and ate in their presence" (Lk 24:43). A spirit cannot eat. The Risen One is a man of flesh and blood; he can talk and eat; and he can be touched. Jesus has to lead the Disciples progressively through stages in order to make them truly believe in the Resurrection.

Perhaps you have experienced the same doubts as those of the Disciples. Doubts about the Resurrection. Doubts that the Risen One and the Crucified One are the same person. Doubts concerning the bodily reality of the Risen One. Luke seeks to transform the doubts you have into faith. Your doubts are allowed to be. They drive you to deepen your faith and to liberate it from projections and illusions. The Risen One answers your doubts by showing you his hands and feet, and the now transfigured wounds. You can experience the Resurrection by seeing the transformation of your own wounds. The wounds in your hands stand for all the blows you have received, for the hard grip of your father or your mother, for the hands that were withdrawn or refused. Your feet were wounded when someone trod on them, did not stand by you, did not walk with you. At communion the Risen One places himself into your wounded hands, so that the light of his love might shine in your wounds.

May the Risen One dissipate your doubts and lead you to faith and joy, so that you can say with all your heart: "The Lord is truly risen. I, too, have seen the Risen One. He is risen within me. He lives bodily in me and transforms the wounds on my hands and feet, too, so that in them the glory of God might shine forth."

Mary of Magdala

THIRD WEEK OF EASTER

The victory of love over death

(John 20:1f)

At the centre of his Easter narrative John places the figure of Mary of Magdala. From the earliest days, Christian piety has taken this woman to heart. Saint Anselm of Canterbury addressed a prayer to her. He calls her the blessed friend of God, addressing her as the one who is "now with the chosen because you are beloved and are beloved because you are chosen of God". Anselm, in line with an old tradition, equates her with the sinful woman of Luke 7 and with Mary of Bethany, the sister of Martha (Lk 10 and Jn 12). He meditates on the mystery that those who love much are pardoned much, and that to Mary, a sinner, was given the great honour of encountering the Risen One.

Mark and Luke tell us that Jesus cast seven demons out of Mary of Magdala (Mk 16:9 and Lk 8:2). She accompanies Jesus and seems to have been particularly close to him. It is significant that Mary had had seven demons driven from her: she was obviously a woman who was completely torn within herself. She had no identity, no centre from which she could live. We would say today that she was a borderline personality. Many therapists are afraid to take on borderline personalities. They consider that the chances of significant healing are low. Jesus obviously was not afraid of Mary of Magdala. He saw her torn-ness and instability, her abysmal fear; but at the same time he sensed her longing for love. He freed her from the seven demons who prevented her from truly living and loving. Through her encounter with Jesus, Mary rediscovers her dignity as a woman. She comes to herself and discovers her centre; and at that centre there is a great love. Mary of Magdala owes Jesus her existence. Through her encounter with him she becomes as if born anew, and there she experiences how love conquers death and how all that has become frozen inside her is awakened to new life.

John sees Mary of Magdala as the great lover. His Easter narrative contains a reference to a love song from the Song of Songs; it is therefore a love story. In the Song of Songs we read: "Upon my bed at night I sought him whom my soul loves; I sought him, but found him not; I called him, but he gave no answer. I will rise now and go about the city, in the streets and in the squares; I will seek him whom my soul loves. I sought him, but found him not. The sentinels found me, as they went about in the city. Have you seen him whom my soul loves? Scarcely had I passed them, when I found him whom my soul loves. I held him, and would not let him go." (Song 3:1-4) Not without reason is the Song of Songs read at the Passover festival in the Jewish liturgy. Easter is the victory of love over death, and this is precisely how John understands it. Mary of Magdala loved Jesus. Through him and his love she came to life, she discovered her dignity. Augustine and Anselm of Canterbury agree that it was love that drove Mary of Magdala to the tomb early in the morning when it was still dark. Augustine says in a sermon: "Whereas the men went home, the stronger love drew the weaker sex back to the place". And Anselm asks in his prayer: "And more than all this, what can I say, how can I find words to tell, about the burning love with which you sought him, weeping at the sepulchre, and wept for him in your seeking? How he came, who can say how or with what kindness, to comfort you, and made you burn with love still more; how he hid from you when you wanted to see him, and showed himself when you did not think to see him; how he was there all the time you sought him, and how he sought you when, seeking him, you wept." (St Anselm)

The story of Mary of Magdala's search for the Risen One is therefore a love story. She sets off during the night when mourning darkens her heart, in order to look for the one whom her soul loves. And when she does not find the one whom her soul loves, she is filled with grief. Anselm of Canterbury thinks that Mary wept because: "No longer able to speak with you living, at least she could mourn for you dead. So, near to death and hating her own life, she repeats in broken tones the words of life which she had heard from the living. And now, besides all this, even the body which she was glad, in a way, to have kept, she believes to have gone." (St Anselm)

What is your deepest longing? Where does your love drive you? Who is the one whom your soul seeks? When you trust your longing and follow your love unto the end, you will – as John tells us in his Gospel – encounter the Risen One, as did Mary of Magdala. All you have to do is, like Mary, depart in the darkness of your heart, to look for the one whom your soul loves.

• MONDAY •

The heart which loves, believes

(John 20:3-10)

John tells us how Mary, as soon as she sees that the stone had been rolled away from the tomb, runs to Simon Peter and to the Disciple whom Jesus loved, and says: "They have taken the Lord out of the tomb, and we do not know where they have laid him." (Jn 20:2) John uses these words three times in the course of this narrative. There is no faith in the Resurrection in her words, only disappointment because she has not found the body. She clearly needs the dead body of Jesus to show her love and to mourn at his side. For Augustine the main reason for her pain was "that she did not know where she should go to find consolation in her pain".

Now an Easter race begins. Simon and John, the Beloved Disciple, run to the tomb. John is faster than Peter and arrives first, but he lets the older man enter before him. Peter enters the tomb. According to John, Peter perceives merely the physical reality: "He saw the linen wrappings lying there, and the cloth that had been on Jesus' head, not lying with the linen wrappings but rolled up in a place by itself." (John 20:6f) He sees, but he does not understand; he cannot imagine why the tomb is empty; all he can do is to establish that Mary of Magdala's report is correct. But he does not understand the significance of the facts. In John's Gospel Peter stands for the person who is led by their reason and will. Those who want to judge everything from the head cannot comprehend the mystery of the Resurrection.

The other disciple, the Beloved Disciple, whom Tradition equates with John, enters the tomb after Peter, "and he saw and believed" (Jn 20:8). John sees with the heart. And a loving heart understands and believes. The Gospel does not tell us what it is exactly that John believed. But the next clause shows that obviously something of the mystery of the Resurrection must have become clear to him, "for as yet they did not know the scripture, that he must rise from the dead" (Jn 20:9). One cannot believe in the Resurrection through reason alone. One needs, like John, a heart that loves and that knows itself to be loved, because the Beloved Disciple is not only the disciple who loves Jesus, but also, as the Gospel always says, "the disciple whom Jesus loved". Whoever knows themselves to be loved by Jesus, can believe in the Resurrection. Such people trust that love is stronger than death, that love will outlive death and will touch them even beyond death.

Neither Peter nor John encounter the Risen One: to Mary of Magdala alone it is given. Only the woman who has loved passionately, who has given herself in her love, may see the Risen One and talk to him. Mary of Magdala is not only the sinner, but also the great lover. Jacobus de Voragine interpreted Jesus' words from Luke's Gospel, that she was pardoned many sins because she loved much, as follows: "And this is she, that same Mary Magdalene to whom our Lord gave so many great gifts. And showed so great signs of love, that he took from her seven devils. He embraced her all in his love, and made her right familiar with him... and he oft times excused her sweetly; for he excused her against the Pharisee which said that she was not clean, and unto her sister that said she was idle, unto Judas, who said that she was a wastresse of goods. And when he saw her weep he could not withhold his tears. And for the love of her he raised Lazarus which had been four days dead." (Voragine) There is probably no other female saint around whom so many legends have been spun. In the figure of Mary Magdalene many have perceived the mystery of the Resurrection. She loved greatly, and she was loved by Jesus in a special way. Because she showed this love beyond death, she was rewarded by her encounter with the Risen One. And through her encounter with Jesus she became a source of love herself. According to a legend, she was driven to southern France together with her brother Lazarus, where she preached to the people, who converted to Christ fascinated by her beauty. Then she lived for thirty years as a hermit and was raised into heaven by the angels each prayer time, so that she could take part in the heavenly liturgy. At an Easter feast she went to church early in the morning, led by the angels. There she received Holy Communion, and her face shone like the sun. When she died after receiving Holy Communion, "there issued out of the body an odour so sweet-smelling that it remained there by the space of seven days to all them that entered in." (Voragine) Thus in her death the mystery of the Resurrection of Jesus was brought to fulfilment.

Is there a side of you that resembles Peter? Can

you also find a John and a Mary Magdalene in you? In what areas of your life does your head dominate your vision? Do you use your heart when you meet people? Are you able to love as passionately as Mary of Magdala does? Or have you never allowed yourself to love passionately because it does not fit in with your Christian upbringing? Trust your love and let yourself be accompanied by Mary Magdalene, in order to be initiated into the mystery of the love which conquers death.

• TUESDAY •

Called by your name

(John 20:11-16)

John describes in a masterly way how Mary Magdalene's mourning is transformed into joy. While Peter and John return home, Mary remains at the tomb. She wants to remain near the place where her beloved Lord was buried, and to weep. "As she wept, she bent over to look into the tomb; and she saw two angels in white, sitting where the body of Jesus had been lying, one at the head and the other at the feet. They said to her, 'Woman, why are you weeping?' She said to them, 'They have taken away my Lord, and I do not know where they have laid him.'" (Jn 20:11-13) So full of grief is she that she dares to enter the chamber of the tomb. But she is so caught up in her grief that even the two angels in shining garments are unable to draw her from her mourning. The angels lovingly ask her for the reason for her sadness. But she only repeats what she has already told the Disciples: "They have taken away my Lord." She talks of her Lord as if he belonged to her. The dead body at least, she feels, should belong to her, since she cannot possess the living one. She grieves because she does not have the body of her beloved to remind her of him. Because she is not afraid to mourn, she is led to her beloved Lord.

After pouring out her troubles to the angels, she 'turns about', as the Greek text puts it in a slightly roundabout way. The encounter with the angels makes her turn about, turn around. She has experienced a turnaround within herself. She turns back. Because she turns back and allows herself to be transformed, she now sees Jesus standing there. But she does not recognise him. Jesus addresses her lovingly, just as the two angels did, asking, "Woman, why are you weeping?" (Jn 20:15). And again she pours out her sorrows to what appears to be the gardener. She wants to see the body of Jesus, touch it, weep over it. But not even that is granted her. "Sir, if you have carried him away, tell me where you have laid him, and I will take him away." (Jn 20:15) She is so fixated on the dead body of Jesus that she does not perceive the living one. It is only when Jesus addresses her by her name that she recognises him and responds with the familiar title 'Rabbuni'. She calls him 'My Master'. Because she has been addressed by her name a new relationship is created. No longer is Jesus just the master of all people, but her master, to whom she knows herself to be tied through her love. In those two words,

'Mary' – 'My Master', the mystery of Resurrection happens. Her mourning is transformed, her eyes are opened, and she recognises the one who is the object of all her love, the one by whom she knows herself to be understood and loved in her deepest being. Jesus has obviously touched her in the very depths of her heart. His word of love has touched her and enabled her to believe that love is stronger than death and that even death cannot overcome the beloved to whom she owes her life.

In one of his prayers Anselm of Canterbury has expressed this encounter between Jesus and Mary Magdalene very movingly: "And so it is; for love's sake / he cannot bear her grief for long or go on hiding himself. / For the sweetness of love he shows himself / who would not for the bitterness of tears. / The Lord calls his servant by the name she has often heard / and the servant by the name she has often heard and the servant knows the voice of her own Lord. / I think, or rather I am sure, / that she responded to the gentle tone / with which he was accustomed to call, 'Mary'. / What joy filled that voice, so gentle and full of love. / He could not have put it more simply and clearly: / 'I know who you are and what you want; / behold me; / do not weep, behold me; / I am he whom you seek.' / At once the tears are changed; / I do not believe that they stopped at once, / but where once they were wrung / from a heart broken and self-tormenting / they flow now from a heart exulting." (St Anselm) The contemplation of the encounter between the Risen One and Mary Magdalene ignites in Anselm the love of Christ, and he seeks with his prayer to awaken love of the Risen One in many people. For Anselm, there is no better way to get in touch with the love that is stronger than death, than through the contemplation of this Easter encounter.

Today, meditate on this wonderful scene and let yourself be initiated by it into the mystery of love! Imagine that Jesus, whose love for you was fulfilled on the cross, now turns to you in this incomprehensible love and calls out your name and speaks directly to you! You are important to him, through his love he brings you to fulfilment, he loves you without reservation, without condition. Your name is written indelibly on his hand. May the meditation on this Easter encounter dispel your deep-seated doubts about yourself and your worth. If you know yourself to be loved wholly and fully, as Mary of Magdala did, then you will no longer feel the need to search for recognition in all places. The experience of Jesus' unconditional love, which outlasts even death, will fill you with a deep inner peace. In his love your longing finds its resting place.

• WEDNESDAY •

Do not hold on to me!

(John 20:17)

It is clear from the Scripture verse for today that Mary of Magdala went towards Jesus full of love and touched him lovingly, or that she was about to embrace him. Artists' representations vary. Sometimes Mary of Magdalene kneels down before Jesus and embraces his feet; on other pictures she touches his side. She wants to embrace him. Whatever the case, her desire is to enter into the same relationship that she had with Jesus before his death. She wants to be able to sense the beloved master and feel his closeness. Since his loving closeness has made her healthy, she now hopes that being close to him once again will transform her mourning into lasting joy and console her forever. But Jesus replies, "Do not hold on to me" (Jn 20:17). Though resurrected Jesus does not simply return to the state in which he was before his death. He is on the way to the Father. Mary cannot hold on to him. The love of the Risen One is no longer transmitted through touch and embrace, but through the uttering of his name, through the deep encounter between the one who has passed through the horror of death and the one who owes her existence to him. Jesus' love for Mary of Magdala was not brought to an end by death. Death could not harm it. The death of Jesus has taught Mary Magdalene to let go of the beloved. It has transformed her love and freed it from all desire to cling.

John understands Jesus Christ's redemption of humankind as an enabling to love. For John the misery of humankind consists in the fact that people have become alienated from themselves. As a result, they have become incapable of love. Whoever is not in touch with themselves, cannot touch another in love. Such a person claims love from others; they use the other's love in order to get a sense of themselves; they suck in all the love that they can get. But there will not be a flowing back and forth of love. Anyone who has become alienated from him- or herself is no longer able to feel the love that flows to them from God; consequently, they do not feel any love for God. The flow of love has run dry. Jesus' death on the cross is for John a sign of the love with which Jesus loved us and brought us to fulfilment. The cross is an initiation into the mystery of divine love. Jesus' love for us is fulfilled in his Resurrection. In the death of Jesus we see that love knows how to renounce, in the Resurrection the victory of love is revealed. This is why John describes the encounter between Jesus and Mary of Magdala as a love story. The cry, "Do not hold on to me!" refers to the love song of the bride who has finally found the one whom her soul loves: "I held him, and would not let him go until I brought him into my mother's house, and into the chamber of her that conceived me. I adjure you, O daughters of Jerusalem, by the gazelles or the wild does: do not stir up or awaken love until it is ready!" (Song 3:4f)

The love which the Risen One shows us and into which he wants to initiate us through his Resurrection, is different from the erotic love between bride and groom. It does not grasp and cannot itself be grasped. Erotic love embraces the beloved and holds them fast. The love of the Risen One sets us free and lets us go. It flows into the depth of our hearts when Christ addresses us lovingly by our name, when he looks at us and turns his face to us. But we cannot reserve this love for ourselves alone. It is a love that is addressed to everyone who will allow themselves to become involved with the risen Christ, as Mary of Magdala had to learn. And as John shows us, she learnt it. The legends have continued John's interpretation further, by describing Mary Magdalene as the great lover, who ponders on the love of God so deeply that her face is nothing but love. Whoever encounters her, is fascinated by her love. Contemplation of the Resurrection initiates us, too, into the mystery of divine love – a love full of eros, as Mary Magdalene shows us, but one which has passed through the transformation of death and does not hold us fast or tie us down to any specific feeling. To this love, which becomes visible in the Resurrection, the words in the Songs of Song apply: "for love is strong as death, passion fierce as the grave. Its flashes are flashes of fire, a raging flame. Many waters cannot quench love, neither can floods drown it. If one offered for love all the wealth of his house, it would be utterly scorned." (Song 8:6f)

How do you deal with your longing to love and to be loved? Do you have doubts about your friend's love, about that of your parents or your spouse? There is no need to suppress your doubts. Let them be. They are there to lead you, through the love that you receive from others, on to the love that flows to you from the Risen One. You can only really enjoy human love if you allow it to flow into the eternal and absolute love of Jesus, the love which has conquered death. To celebrate the Resurrection means that we believe in the love that does not fade even in death, that we know ourselves to be loved by the eternal love of God.

Accepted into the love of God

(John 20:17)

The reason why Mary of Magdala must not hold on to Jesus is that he has not yet ascended to the Father. John understands Resurrection as the ascent to the Father. When Jesus became man he came down among us humans. At the cross he is raised up by the Father and glorified. In the Resurrection he ascends to the Father. Then, coming from the Father, he will reveal himself as the Crucified, Risen and Glorified One. The question is: what does John's concept of the Resurrection actually mean for us? Is it merely a theological construct, and can we live from it?

During Eastertide the Gospel on weekdays is often taken from the Last Supper discourses (Jn 14-17). Where Jesus repeatedly says that he will go to the Father in order to prepare a mansion for us: "I am going away, and I am coming to you. If you loved me, you would rejoice that I am going to the Father, because the Father is greater than I. And now I have told you this before it occurs, so that when it does occur, you may believe." (Jn 14:28f) Jesus goes to the Father in the Resurrection. This should be a reason for the Disciples to rejoice.

The one with whom they have lived, whom they have touched and felt, is now in the glory of the Father. And we, within our own selves, now have an intercessor with the Father. In him, part of us is already with God. We have already been raised to heaven with Jesus Christ, and in him, we are immersed in the love between Father and Son. It is a recurring theme of the farewell discourses at the Last Supper that the Father loves the Son and the Son the Father, and that we are able to participate in this love. In the priestly prayer Jesus asks that the love with which the Father has loved him, may also be in us and that Christ himself be in us (Jn 17:26).

For John, through the Resurrection we are raised up into the glory of the Father, we have risen to heaven in Christ and we have been taken up into the love between the Father and the Son. The Resurrection is thus not only a statement about Jesus Christ, but about us as Christians. The Resurrection enables us Christians to be different, to live differently. True life, life which actually deserves the name, according to John's Gospel, becomes possible only where divine life flows into humankind. Divine life is for John always also divine love. Because divine love flows within us, we are able to love one another. And only love makes life worth living.

Think about the love that you have for other people! How does this love feel? What does it do to you? Imagine that the love which flows within you is not limited to this or that person; imagine that in the love you have, God's love flows within you; imagine that it leads you into God and introduces you to the everlasting love between the Father and the Son. Perhaps this will help you to understand what John means when he writes, "God is love, and those who abide in love abide in God, and God abides in them." (1 Jn 4:16) Love is the place where we experience God and experience ourselves in a new manner; in it we sense the mystery of our life; through it our life becomes worth loving; in it we are accepted in God's love, taken into his heart.

• FRIDAY •

I have seen the Lord

(John 20:18)

Jesus instructs Mary of Magdala to tell the Disciples to "go to my brothers and say to them, 'I am ascending to my Father and your Father, to my God and your God.'" (Jn 20:17) Her mission is to announce the mystery of the Resurrection, as John understands it, to the Disciples. The task of announcing the Resurrection is given to a woman. John is here making a bold statement, one that without doubt made an impression on the Early Church. For this reason, Augustine calls Mary of Magdala, 'apostola apostolorum' – the apostle of the apostles'. It is asking a lot from the Disciples' circle of men to accept that a woman should announce the Resurrection – but that this woman should be, of all people, the sinner and the woman from whom Jesus drove seven demons, probably represents an even greater challenge for the church of men. The Early Church saw in Mary of Magdala an image of the many women who played an important role in the spreading of the faith. In her, it discerned the mystery of the Jesus' message: Jesus calls on sinners, and on sinners in particular, to follow him and to witness to him before the whole world.

Mary of Magdala announces to the Disciples what Jesus has told her. But she goes further and includes her own witness: "I have seen the Lord" (Jn 20:18). She has not only heard the words of the Risen One, she has seen and experienced him, she has encountered him. In her encounters with Jesus she began to understand the mystery of her own life. She shares with the Disciples what she herself has experienced. She starts with her own experience rather than by making objective statements. Her approach gives us a clear indication of how we ourselves, should talk about the Resurrection. It is not enough to repeat what others say about the Resurrection: we must start with ourselves and our own experience. Theology is no abstract edifice of ideas, but an interpretation of the experience which each one of us has of him- or herself and of God. If we ponder on our own lives, we too will realise that we have seen the Lord and can witness to this fact. We see the Lord in the poor and sick, in those suffering hardship and in strangers. We see the Risen One in the person who talks to us and touches us in the depths of our heart. We see the Risen One in all we have experienced in our lives, in apparent coincidences, in that which once broken is re-formed again; in that which once considered improbable, now becomes reality. We see the Risen One everywhere where God's majesty shines forth: in the liturgy, in the beauty of nature, in the music that makes the hitherto unheard-of resound, and in painting which makes the invisible visible. We encounter the Risen One where God's light shines in a person, where the mystery of God blossoms in a flower.

Mary Magdala witnessed to the Resurrection in the only way possible: when we talk, we must learn to come from where we are, from our own experience of Resurrection. In meditating on Mary of Magdala's story we will find many resonances with our own lives and will be able to say with her, "I have seen the Lord".

Today, carry the word, 'I have seen the Lord' with you. You will look at other people with fresh eyes. You will have a different perspective on the day's events. And perhaps you will recognise that there is more to your everyday life than just duty and performance, than effort and a sense of feeling overwhelmed. The Resurrection can be experienced in the everyday: something new breaking forth, God breaking into your world. When God breaks into your world, you experience healing and wholeness right there amid the turbulence of your everyday life; and the Resurrection will happen there, in the midst of death.

• SATURDAY •

Sent to the people

(Acts 8:26-40)

On the Thursday of the third week of Easter, we read the story of the baptism of the Ethiopian, another one of Luke's typical Resurrection stories. Luke's purpose is to show us how the Resurrection can be experienced when people of different origin encounter one another. The angel of the Lord appears. The Acts of the Apostles frequently mentions angels of the Resurrection; the angels give witness to the fact that Christ is alive and that he is the true Messiah: "Then an angel of the Lord said to Philip, 'Get up and go toward the south to the road that goes down from Jerusalem to Gaza.'" (Acts 8:26) Philip departs and walks down this lonely road. He does not know what awaits him. Then the angel of the Lord orders him to follow the chariot on which an Ethiopian court official is driving home: "So Philip ran up to it and heard him reading the prophet Isaiah. He asked, 'Do you understand what you are reading?' He replied, 'How can I, unless someone guides me?' And he invited Philip to get in and sit beside him." (Acts 8:30f) Philip gets into the chariot and explains to him the passage where the prophet Isaiah talks about the servant of God, who is led to slaughter like a lamb.

Using this passage as a starting point, Philip announces the Gospel of Jesus. The chamberlain is so fascinated by this that he orders the chariot to stop at the next watering place and asks to be baptised. No sooner has the chamberlain been baptised than Philip is carried away by the spirit of the Lord, and the chamberlain can no longer see him.

Luke's description of the scene is similar to that which he used for the Emmaus disciples. But it is not now the Risen One himself who appears to disappointed disciples, but Philip. Philip announces the news of the Resurrection to a foreigner who has come to Jerusalem on a pilgrimage. The chamberlain was obviously a seeker after God. But he had not yet found the true God. He was still torn, as the Emmaus disciples had been. He had no one to talk to. He was reading aloud a prophesy from Isaiah. But because an angel of the Lord placed Philip by his side, his eyes were opened and he received new life in baptism. There is always Resurrection when the angel of the Lord sends us to open someone's eyes. The path of transformation asks of us, initially, that we accompany the other. Philip first follows the chamberlain and then listens closely to what he is reading and to what moves him. Then he asks him whether he actually understands what he is reading. In our case, this question might be something like: "Do you understand what has happened to you? Can you explain to yourself why you have chosen this particular course, why we are meeting at this particular time? What touches you in this book, or what fascinates you about this music?" When our questions strike a chord in the other person, then begins the process which leads to Resurrection, then we can celebrate the Resurrection.

To whom does the Angel of the Resurrection want to send you today? Who should you accompany on their path? When should you listen carefully to what a person close to you is trying to express? Where should you probe when someone talks to you about their experiences, of their dreams or of a book that they are reading? In fairytales it is always important to ask the right question. What question would you like to ask your life companion, your companion on the road? Is there a question that could unlock the mystery of that person's life and lead them to an experience of the Risen One?

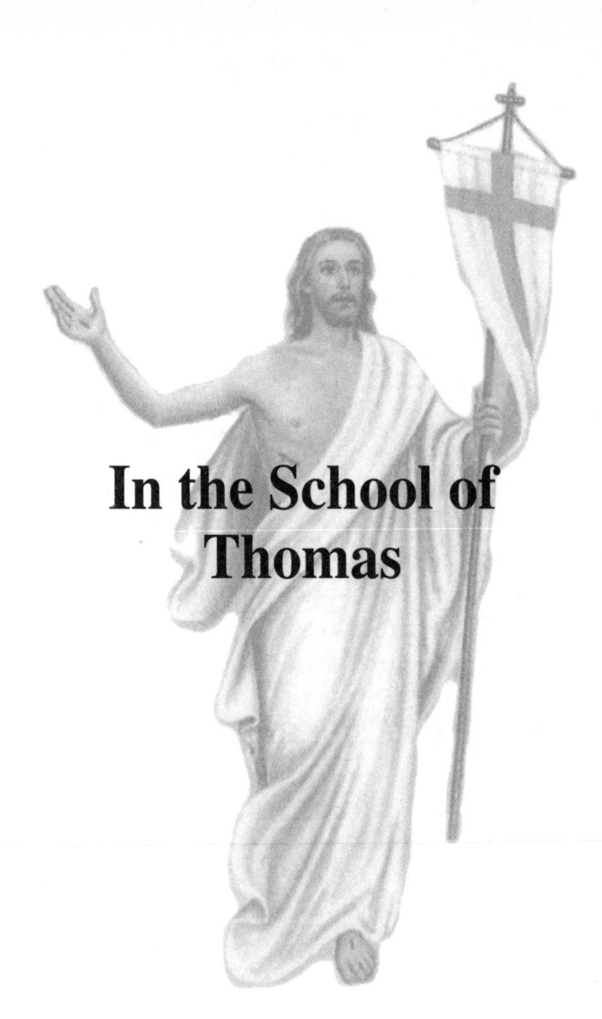

In the School of Thomas

FOURTH WEEK OF EASTER

• SUNDAY •

The closed door of my heart

(John 20:19)

"When it was evening on that day, the first day of the week, and the doors of the house where the disciples had met were locked for fear of the Jews, Jesus came and stood among them and said, 'Peace be with you.'" (Jn 20:19) The Risen One passes through locked doors. The Disciples' fear cannot stop him from coming to them through the barred doors and wishing them peace. This is a beautiful image of the Resurrection. All too often we have locked our doors to others. We let no one enter. We hide, encasing ourselves within our fear. Resurrection means that no lock and no bar can stop the Risen One from coming within and touching our heart. And no Christian community which shuts itself off from others can stop the Risen One himself from stepping into its midst and transforming it.

In many fairytales and legends the door is an important symbol of human 'self-becoming'. Jesus says the same of himself in the Gospel for Good Shepherd Sunday: "I am the gate. Whoever enters by me will be saved, and will come in and go out and find pasture." (Jn 10:9) Jesus not only enters through our locked doors, he himself is the door through which we can come to life. The door is a symbol of the transition from one area to another: from this life to the other life, from the profane to the sacred, for example. In the Middle Ages the entrance doors to cathedrals were always decorated with the figure of Christ enthroned. At that time people still knew that only through Christ can we gain access to true life. Only when we take Jesus' words seriously does our life become whole and healed, and we can come to our true self – when we step through the door that is Jesus. Jesus used two images to illustrate what this means: we will go in and out, and we will find a pasture. Life will stream back and forth in us. We will no longer be closed in on ourselves, going round in circles. Neither will we live only at the surface. In dreams we sometimes cannot find the door that leads into our house: an image that infallibly tells us that we have no access to our heart, to our own self, that we walk around outside, that we are not in touch with our soul. When we enter through the door which is Christ, then we will go in and out; then we will be in touch with our own heart and at the same time we will help to shape this world. We will find pasture. We will find the food that truly nourishes us.

Christ as the true door, is a beautiful image of the Resurrection. We can lock our doors as much as we like, Christ as the door to life will break open the locked doors of our hearts and walk through them. When he so comes to us, we are able to connect with our own inner self.

Today, make a conscious effort to look at the doors through which you walk! Some doors are beautifully made. Doors lead into freedom. Step through them and leave the stuffy air of your office behind. Other doors open onto rooms where you feel at ease, large and beautiful rooms, airy, flooded with light, tastefully decorated. Take these rooms as an image of the rooms in the house of your life! And imagine that you lead the Risen One through all the rooms in your house, so that all that has been locked is unlocked and all that has been cast aside and repressed can come back to life! Have you ever had a dream in which doors played an important role? Which door should you choose, which door would lead to a life with greater breadth; which door would lead you to that room which is right for you, as you are now? Which door is waiting for you to open it?

• MONDAY •

Peace be with you!

(John 20:19-21)

On two consecutive occasions the Risen Christ wishes the Disciples peace. (Jn 20:19 and 21) This is unusual. When John describes the scene on Easter night he reflects the Eucharistic practice of the early Christians. The bishop invariably opened the feast with the salutation, 'Peace be with you'; thus all believers knew that the Risen One himself was among them. Following his greeting the Risen Christ talks to the Disciples and brings his love to fulfilment in them, love which has become visible in the death and Resurrection of Jesus. The words of John's Gospel are the words of the Lord who has risen and has been lifted up. Christ used these words when he talked to his Disciples before ascending to the Father. With the same words he now addresses us. They are words which come from the glory of the Father and which now reach us where we are. They are words of love, cancelling the limits imposed by death, joining heaven and earth.

The Eucharist can be understood using the two images of Easter night that John presents to us: "After he said this, he showed them his hands and his side." (Jn 20:20) The Risen One not only talks to us when we are gathered to break bread, but also shows us his hands and his side with its wounds. His pierced hands tell us that he has put his hands into the flames and pulled us out, that he has acted for us and has held his hand over us in protection. He has borne on our behalf the wounds that pierce our hands. The wounds in his hands are a reminder of all the blows we have received from others, of the hands which grasp us tightly, which refuse to let us go, which hold us down, pin us down, hurt us. When someone refuses to take our hand or withdraws theirs, our hands are wounded. In each Eucharist Jesus offers to take our wounds upon himself, for them to be cut into his own hand. Buddhism, too, uses the imagery of the open hand: Buddha's open hand is a symbol of how he holds no secrets back; and so Jesus' hands show the Disciples that he has revealed everything to them. By showing us his hands in the Eucharist, he tells us that we are his friends: "I have called you friends, because I have made known to you everything that I have heard from my Father." (Jn 15:15)

In the Eucharist Jesus holds his pierced side out to us. From his side blood and water flow towards us. The water and the blood are for John an image of the Holy Spirit that is poured out over us and of the love of Christ which is poured into us. In the Eucharist we drink from the chalice the blood of Jesus and in his blood the love of God, which has been made man. We take his body in our hand so that through his body the wounds in our hands may be healed. And from the chalice we drink the blood which pours from his side for us, so that the love of Christ with which he has brought us to fulfilment, may permeate everything in us and transform it. We are called to respond like the Disciples to the mystery of the love which is made visible for us in the hands and the side of the Risen One: "Then the disciples rejoiced when they saw the Lord." (Jn 20:20) In the body and blood of the Eucharist we behold the Lord himself.

The second image that John uses for the Eucharist on Easter Night, is contained in the following words of Jesus: "As the Father has sent me, so I send you." (Jn 20:21) To experience the Resurrection is to be sent out. It is not enough to just rejoice in the presence of the Risen One. The Risen One sends us out into the world so that we may pass on his words and continue to give witness to his love. Through us Christ wants to enter into all the areas of this world. Through us he wants to pass through the closed doors of those who have withdrawn into themselves out of fear. Through us he wants to show the people his hands and his side. Through our hands he wants to touch the people tenderly, encourage them and raise them up. Jesus wants us to use our hands to do his work and act for the benefit of humankind. And through our hearts Jesus wants to show his pierced side to all people. Through our hearts he desires to pour his love into the isolation and loneliness of people.

What would you like to take in hand today? Whom would you like to touch tenderly, to whom stretch our your hand in reconciliation? To whom do you want to show your heart, your love, your goodwill? Pay close attention to your heart: when you are with people, is your heart closed and tight, or is it open and wide? Imagine that the Risen Christ wants to show his love to the people through your heart!

• TUESDAY •

Jesus breathes his love into us

(John 20:22f)

"When he had said this, he breathed on them and said to them, 'Receive the Holy Spirit. If you forgive the sins of any, they are forgiven them; if you retain the sins of any, they are retained.'" (Jn 20:22f) Jesus breathes on his Disciples and, in this tender manner, gives them his spirit. The gift is, in fact, his personal spirit, from which he lived, in which he acted, talked and loved. When he breathes his spirit into us, we are able to talk and act and love in the same way as he did. The spirit which he breathes into us is the Holy Spirit. But at the same time this spirit is his personal spirit, his particular way of approaching people and talking to them. It is his personal charism that he passes on to us.

Breathing on another person in this sense means that you give them the innermost thing that you possess. Jesus breathes his love onto us. And so when we breathe we breathe more than mere air, we breathe the Spirit of God, the love of God. The Persian mystic Jalal al-din Rumi calls the breath, 'God's scent of love', which permeates us through and through. There is probably no more intense communion between Jesus and ourselves than when he so breathes his love into us. In each breath we are able to perceive his love in bodily form. Once we open our senses and feel our way into this breath in all its fullness, we begin to perceive Christ's scent of love that flows through us in each breath. This helps us to get a sense of the intimacy that exists between Jesus and ourselves, an intimacy the intensity of which could hardly be surpassed.

The word for 'to breathe in', 'emphysao', is used in the Greek text of Genesis to describe God's act of creation. God's breath awakens life in all creation. Thus Jesus' breathing onto us is an act of creation. Jesus creates a new reality in us through his Spirit. And this new reality is the love that permeates us. For John, love is expressed above all in the forgiveness of sins. Here we do not mean the forgiveness which we receive from God, but that which we humans extend to each other. The ability to forgive someone who has hurt me is for John an expression of the presence of the Holy Spirit which the Risen One has breathed into me. When I am unable to forgive another, I am not really free of them, and I am filled with anger, hurt and sadness inside. The other person determines my mood. When Christ's love permeates me in my breath, I am able to forgive the other person. They no longer have any power over me. Sin separates people from each other, it alienates them from the community and makes them turn in on themselves. Forgiving love makes the divided person whole and receives them back into the community. Life is then able to flow in that person again, and love is able to stream through them.

Pay attention to your breath today! Imagine that you breathe in the Spirit of Jesus with every breath, that in your breath the love of Christ permeates every pore of your body. How does that make you feel? What flavour does your life take on as a result? When this love becomes your inner reality, forgiveness is no longer an overwhelming demand, or even just a demand. You let go of the hurt caused by the other because love flows through you and there is no room left inside you for bitterness. You will experience how the love which is forgiveness liberates you from the power of the people who have hurt you. The forgiveness of which you are able to grant because Christ's love within you heals your wounded past. You no longer live out of the hurts of your life story, but from the reality of the love which flows through you in your breath.

• WEDNESDAY •

Seeking the experience

(John 20:24-27)

Using the figure of Thomas, John shows us how our faith in the Resurrection can grow through any doubts we may feel. From time immemorial the figure of Thomas has exerted a fascination on people. Thomas has often been seen as the doubter. Since our faith is shaken by doubt time and again, we can easily recognise ourselves in Thomas. We feel in tune with him. He is truly our twin, and he represents what we ourselves feel. But let us look a little more closely at the way in which John interprets Thomas' behaviour. Thomas was not present when Jesus appeared to the Disciples on Easter Sunday night and when he breathed the Holy Spirit into them. When the Disciples tell him about it, he is not satisfied. He replies: "Unless I see the mark of the nails in his hands, and put my finger in the mark of the nails and my hand in his side, I will not believe." (Jn 20:25)

In actual fact, Thomas is not a doubter, but someone who seeks experience. He does not content himself with just believing what others tell him. He wants to see, feel, touch for himself. Only then is he prepared to believe. John invites us to go to the school of Thomas and to learn faith in the Resurrection as he did. Our faith needs experience. Our dignity won't allow us to believe only what others tell us is true. Our wish to experience God, to experience the Resurrection is justified. But if we want to sense the miracle of love at work in us, we must open ourselves to receive the very different and unexpected response that Jesus gives, as Thomas did.

The condition that Thomas gives for his faith is strangley touching. Why does Thomas place such emphasis on the wounds of Jesus, on the marks of the nails on his hands and in his open side? Can he only believe in the Resurrection if he touches the wounds of Jesus? Does he need the evidence to prove that the Risen One and the Crucified One are one and the same, because it is in his opinion so very unlikely that the one who has died in such agony, will ever live again? It would seem that, quite naturally, the entirely unexpected and agonising death of Jesus on the cross has shaken Thomas' faith in the Messiah so deeply that he requires a tangible proof to enable him to believe in the Resurrection.

Eight days after the Easter Saturday night the Disciples are gathered together again, again behind closed doors. Eight is the figure of infinity, of eternity. The eighth day is the Day of the Resurrection, which knows no night. It is, however, also the Sunday when Christians gather for the Eucharist. At the end of the first century, when John wrote his Gospel, Christians often gathered behind closed doors, because they were frightened of persecution by the Roman authorities. These closed doors are an image of those who still live in fear, who – despite the encounter with the Risen One on Easter night – do not yet have a trusting faith. With the greeting, "Peace be with you!", Jesus comes and stands among the Disciples, as he does every Sunday when Christians meet to break bread and gather round the Risen One. Through Thomas John wants to show us how we, who celebrate the Eucharist Sunday after Sunday, can learn to believe in the presence of the Risen One.

Jesus granted Thomas what he had refused to Mary Magdalene: he allowed him to touch his hands and his side. On Easter Night he only showed the Disciples his hands and his side; now he asks Thomas to place his fingers in the wounds on his hands and to touch the wound in his side with his hand. In the Eucharist Jesus is not only in our midst: he also allows us to touch him. When he puts his body into our hands in the shape of the bread, then we place our finger into his wound, because it is his flesh, which he has given up for us, which he has given up for the life of the world (cf. Jn 6:51). When we drink from the cup, we drink the blood that flows from the wound in his side. Then the same happens to us as happened to Thomas. If, believing, we place our fingers into the wounds in his hands and into the wound in his side, then these wounds can produce the same miracle of faith. Then his promise from the Eucharistic discourse on the bread of life comes true: "Those who eat my flesh and drink my blood abide in me, and I in them." (Jn 6:56) In this discourse John used the word 'trogon', which means 'to eat', 'to gnaw', 'to chew', 'to crunch', and also 'to eat raw fruit, vegetables or nuts'. It is therefore a pleasurable eating, which involves all the senses. In this chewing I truly touch the flesh of the Risen One. I touch the very wounds in which the miracle of his love occurred. The wounds are for John a sign of the love with which Jesus has given himself up for his friends. For John, eating the Eucharistic bread, the bread which comes from heaven, with all the senses, is like a kiss of love in which we taste the love of the beloved in all its fullness. And when we drink the wine, the blood that flows from his side, then we are able to say with the bridegroom in the Song of Songs: "how much better is your love than wine" (Song 4:10). But we can only perceive this love in the bread and in the wine, in the body and blood of Christ, if we are not unbelievers, but believers; if we believe that the Risen One is truly among us and that he really touches us in his flesh and blood.

What experience can your fait call upon? Where has doubt deepened your faith and liberated it from illusions? What does it mean to you to place your finger in the wounds of Jesus? Where have you experienced the Risen One and where have you touched him?

• THURSDAY •

The personal confession

(John 20:28)

Thomas responds to Jesus' offer to touch his wounds by uttering the confession, "My Lord and my God!" (Jn 20:28) This utterance constitutes the clearest statement of belief in Jesus' Godhead found in John's Gospel. Back in the first chapter of his Gospel, John describs the calling of the Disciples in a clever manner, showing how the Disciples gain an ever-clearer insight into the mystery of Jesus. The first two disciples address him as follows: "'Rabbi' (which translated means Teacher), 'where are you staying?'" (Jn 1:38) Andrew says to Simon: "We have found the Messiah" (which is translated as Anointed). (Jn 1:41) Nathaniel, who initially – very much like Thomas – has his doubts about whether anything good can come out of Nazareth, finally confesses, after Jesus seems to have read his thoughts: "Rabbi, you are the Son of God! You are the King of Israel!" (Jn 1:49) In the chapter dealing with the Resurrection John returns to these confessions. Here, too, the Evangelist highlights the reactions of individual people: first Mary Magdalene from the circle of women, and then Thomas from the circle of the Disciples. It is not the community as such which is able to believe. Faith is always a matter for the individual, each person must come to realise for themselves who God is and who this Jesus of Nazareth is.

In the final passages of John's Gospel the increasing intensity of the personal confessions is expressed by the word 'my'. While the first Disciples address Jesus as Rabbi, Mary of Magdala says: "Rabbuni – my Master". Jesus is not just any Rabbi, albeit one who excels all others, he is her Rabbi. In his words, his wounds and in his death he has proved himself to be the Rabbi whom she can address as 'my Master'. This 'my' expresses a deep relationship, a relationship of tender love, a relationship which has grown through experience, through encounters, through words and deeds of love. In a similar way Thomas takes up Nathaniel's confession: "You are the Son of God". But he, too, adds the word 'my': "My Lord and my God". It is not a theological statement, which correctly reflects the credal truth of the Church: it is a personal confession that comes from experience. And here, too, it is the experience of love that urges Thomas to make this statement. The fact that Jesus lovingly responded to Thomas' rather pre-emptory demand to touch his hands and his side, is for Thomas the sign of a love that is able to transform all, even those who doubt or who do not believe.

Write down your personal profession of faith today! Do not content yourself with writing what is written down in the Catechism or what you have learnt from others! Try to express what God means to you personally, what Jesus Christ tells you, how you understand the Resurrection! What images and names spring to mind when you think of Jesus? Say these names out aloud and claim them for yourself by adding 'my' before them! Listen with your heart to what you are saying and to how you respond to these names: 'My shepherd, My Lord, My brother, My friend, My physician, My rock, My refuge, My God.' Repeat slowly, in the company of Thomas, the following phrase, "My Lord and my God", and perhaps you will get some idea how, in these words, all the contraries of this world collapse: closeness and distance, love and awe, belief and unbelief, doubt and certainty, touch and non-touch. The remote God becomes your God, the intangible God becomes tangible, the Imperceptible allows himself to be touched by you. Then in love the distance between God and yourself collapses, and you become united with God in Christ.

• FRIDAY •

Not seeing and yet believing

(John 20:29)

John concludes the story of Thomas with the following words of Jesus: "Have you believed because you have seen me? Blessed are those who have not seen and yet have come to believe." (Jn 20:29) Some think that Jesus directs these words to us, who are no longer able to see the Risen One in body and yet are asked to believe. If Thomas is to be an image of our faith we must, however, understand John's words in a different way. The following two things always form part of our faith: we are able to see, experience and touch the Risen One as Thomas did; at the same time, however, we both see and yet don't see him. There are times in our lives when we see and experience nothing. Experience in itself is good and right, and deepens our faith, but we must not bind our faith to experience. We cannot force experience: an integral part of our faith journey, it, too, must frequently cross the desert, the emptiness, the darkness. At those times, we see nothing.

Jesus calls blessed those who do not see and yet believe. Here, he clearly wants to initiate his hearers into an even higher form of faith than hitherto.

Faith transcends experience. Faith is all too often non-experience. But in this non-experience faith nevertheless holds tightly to God, the Invisible and the Intangible. Many believers are familiar with this non-experience. They are trapped in a dark hole. No light seems to shine into their darkness. They suffer from their wounds and feel no transformation and no healing. And yet they believe that they are in God's hand. This situation has nothing to do with the fact that people of our time cannot see Jesus as the Disciples did all those years ago. The problem is a much more fundamental one: there are times in which the promises of the Bible seem empty, in which we experience no healing, no liberation from our fear, no consolation and no consoler, in which we see no light at the end of the tunnel. Those who nevertheless believe amid such darkness, are to be called blessed. For Jesus, such impossible situations are not blessed in themselves. He himself is clearly familiar with such experiences. In his death-battle on the cross, when everything seemed hopeless, he nevertheless believed and held on to God. Large numbers of the Jewish people who were led into the gas chambers held on to God and cried out to him in spite of all their doubts. There is the grace through which – in spite of the fact that we do not see that God is close to us, in spite of the fact that we see no other person being close to us, standing by our side and giving us hope – we nevertheless believe. It is a gift of grace that deep in our heart there is a faith that cannot easily be driven out by events that seem to contradict it. Jesus calls those blessed, who do not see and yet believe. Here John's Gospel gives us the ninth beatitude, the culmination of the eightfold blessedness described in the Sermon on the Mount.

Look out for this beatitude today! Let yourself be initiated into faith by Thomas, who believes even though he does not see. Try to believe in the essential goodness of the person next to you, even though it is hard to see because of all the aggression they emanate. Believe that you are in God's good hand, even though you do not feel it at present. Trust the fact that your illness or the continual ill-health of your neighbour has a meaning, even though you do not understand it. Today, try to behold the invisible in the visible; in the wounds, love; in the hurts, that which is whole; in all that you encounter, an expression of the love of the Risen One! Doing this, you will, like Thomas, touch the one who wants to touch you with his love through all that you touch with attention and care.

• SATURDAY •

The liberating power of prayer

(Acts 12:6-17)

In the Acts of the Apostles Luke tells us what the faith which does not see and yet believes, may look like, and how we can experience Resurrection where we do not expect it. Herod had James executed. When he realised that the Jews were pleased by this action, he also had Peter taken prisoner. Peter, it seemed, did not stand a chance, but "the church prayed fervently to God for him" (Acts 12:5). The community believed even though it did not see anything which suggested that Peter might be saved. Herod was a cruel ruler. He had made himself popular among the people by murdering James, and so he wanted to continue this policy by putting Peter to death. But it was the community, which believed even though it did not see, that triumphed in the end.

"The very night before Herod was going to bring him out, Peter, bound with two chains, was sleeping between two soldiers, while guards in front of the door were keeping watch over the prison. Suddenly an angel of the Lord appeared and a light shone in the cell. He tapped Peter on the side and woke him, saying, 'Get up quickly.' And the chains fell off his wrists." (Acts 12:6f) The angel led Peter out of prison. "Peter went out and followed him; he did not realise that what was happening with the angel's help was real; he thought he was seeing a vision." (Acts 12:9) Only when the angel left him in a narrow street, did Peter come to himself: "Now I am sure that the Lord has sent his angel and rescued me from the hands of Herod and from all that the Jewish people were expecting." (Acts 12:11) When he knocked on the door of the house where he knew many from the community to be gathered, the maid recognised his voice. But the others did not believe her, and they said, "You are out of your mind!" (Acts 12:15) Although they had prayed for Peter to be rescued, they did not believe it when it actually happened. Only when Peter told them how an angel of the Lord led him out of prison, did they believe.

Peter finds himself in a dead-end situation. Chained between soldiers, he does not stand a chance. But with God the impossible becomes possible. Luke's aim in this story is to give courage to Christians, showing them that Resurrection is possible for them too, amid persecution, even in hopeless captivity. The Evangelist extends his encouragement to us, when we seem to be trapped, with no way out. Even if our prison is lightless, even when the shackles of our fear are too strong, even when we seem to stand no chance of breaking free from all that binds us and on which we are dependent, God can still send his angel into any situation, freeing us. We must never lose hope. We must believe in the Resurrection, even when we have never experienced it in ourselves or in our brothers and sisters. For, despite all, the Resurrection is possible. God sends his angel; our shackles simply fall off of their own accord; the soldiers lose their power, they cease to frighten us, we can pass freely between them.

Today the angel of the Lord enters your prison. When you feel that you are a prisoner, shackled, inhibited, blocked, when you are among the soldiers, when the voices of your super-ego are shredding you, he gets you going. Say aloud the angel's words to Peter: "Quick, get up! Gird yourself! Follow me!" Trust the angel who wants to lead you into freedom! And when God wants to send you as an angel into the prison of others, trust him! Give a prod to the brother or sister and encourage them to get up and walk the path that leads to freedom! The doors will open and the power of Herod will collapse. Luke tells how the mighty

Herod is consumed by worms and dies. When we follow the angel who gets us going and leads us into freedom, then the powerful voices of the super-ego are destroyed. They simply dissolve. We are free to go our own way, the way of the Resurrection.

An Early Meal with the Risen One

FIFTH WEEK OF EASTER

• SUNDAY •

The night of emptiness

(John 21:1-5)

The story of Jesus' appearance on the shores of Lake Tiberias illustrates the presence of the Resurrection in everyday life. The disciples have returned to their daily toil. There are seven of them. Seven is the figure of transformation. Seven always means that the earthly becomes connected with the divine, that heaven and earth touch each other. The seven Disciples appear to have been brought together more or less by coincidence. But through the encounter with the Risen One they become a holy community, a community of which Jesus himself becomes the mysterious centre. Suddenly there is a great spirit of togetherness, an atmosphere in which heaven is open above them.

But initially their togetherness appears to be rather in vain. All their actions seem futile – a painful experience shared many people today. Everything appears vain, futile. The disciples are frustrated, disappointed. There is no point. Why bother? Nothing will come of it. Why work on ourselves? We just end up falling back into the same old mistakes. The feeling of futility robs us of the energy which we need to live, and it makes us ill. Futility is an experience which the Bible mentions in many different places. Job experienced futility. He complained that he was labouring in vain (Job 9:29). The consolation of his friends achieved nothing. They comforted him with empty nothings

(Job 21:34). The psalmist in Psalm 73 laments having kept his heart pure in vain (Ps 73:13). The psalmist's whole wrestling with God's will was futile. Evildoers seem to be better off. Why then should the psalmist toil every day? Everything is in vain. All great speeches, all glorious deeds come to nothing: "Surely everyone goes about like a shadow. Surely for nothing they are in turmoil." (Ps 39:7)

Since our deeds seem to be futile, it makes no difference if we follow someone willingly, as the disciples did with their leader Peter. Euphoria alone is not much help. When Peter tells the disciples that he is going fishing, they respond full of enthusiasm: "We will go with you." (Jn 21:3) They hope that Peter will be able to show them how to make their life a success. Many today listen to a self-appointed guru who knows exactly what is what. Fascinated by his charisma, they climb into his boat, hoping that henceforth things will get better. But like the disciples, such people must experience that it is all in vain: "but that night they caught nothing" (Jn 21:3). All is vain. And it is night. They can see nothing in its darkness. Everything seems dark, meaningless. The boat that they share with the guru only takes them further out into the night.

Into this grey morning of futility and desolation steps Jesus. "Just after daybreak, Jesus stood on the beach" (Jn 21:4). If I suffer in the night from the vanity of my labours, I long for the morning. Yet not every morning brings comfort. There are the grey mornings, desolate mornings when we do not want to get up, when we see no meaning in discovering what this day holds for us. But on the shore is Jesus. The Disciples are still in the boat, out on on the lake. They are still in the world of the unconscious, in the world of their nightmares. Jesus steps into their lives from another world. The disciples do not recognise him. But Jesus enters into relationship with them: "My children", he asks them, "have you nothing to eat?" Jesus calls them 'children': they are still ignorant. Although they are experienced fishermen, they have no real understanding of what actually matters in life: and so he shows them a way. He takes them into his school. Their endeavours are truly in vain. They toil for nothing. If they wish their lives to be truly successful, they must take another path. But they will only be able to find these new paths if they admit that they are children, that all their abilities are no use when it comes to what really matters.

In which areas of your life do you experience futility? Where do you feel that everything is meaningless, that everything is in vain? Perhaps all the care you put into your children's upbringing seems pointless. They go completely different ways. They seem to have taken the wrong path. Perhaps your work is in vain. You see no success. You try in vain to become another person. You keep falling back into your old ways. Bring the word of Jesus into your emptiness: 'Child, have you nothing to eat?' Do you have anything which truly nourishes you? Jesus steps onto the shore of your grey morning. He talks to you, that your life today might not be in vain, that today you might make a true success of your life, that it will not lead into emptiness, but become healed and whole.

• MONDAY •

It is the Lord

(John 21:6f)

Jesus issues the frustrated disciples with the following command: "Cast the net to the right side of the boat, and you will find some." (Jn 21:6) The right side is considered in many religions to be the better, the lucky side. Since in Antiquity it was the right arm that bore the weapon, the right side was used as an image of power and success. In psychology the right side is the conscious area, whereas the left is associated with the subconscious. Jesus certainly does not advise the experienced fishermen on how to catch more by improving their technique: he shows them how they can make their lives a true success. The disciples must not trust their own experience alone. They must listen to the one who steps towards them from the shore, who talks to them from another world. The voice of Jesus resounds in their heart with soft, silent suggestions – suggestions which nevertheless show them the way more surely than the methods they are already familiar with. Whoever listens to their inner voice, will hear the voice of Jesus, which reaches from the shore into the night of their unconscious. All too often our vision is blinkered, and we do not recognise the paths that lead to true life.

The disciples are called to become conscious of what it is they are doing, to become aware of their actions. When we act consciously, we are attentive, totally immersed in what we are doing. When we have no ulterior motive – such as, earning as much money as possible, finishing as quickly as possible, or outperforming others – and are simply engaged in 'doing', then our labours will bear fruit. When we act unconsciously, we drift along, we do what we have always done. Conscious doing demands a decision. I make a decision to do what I am doing. And I take responsibility for it. I am also responsible for the mood in which I approach the task. I cannot make any person or circumstance responsible for my resignation or frustration. I make a deliberate choice in favour of whatever it is I am doing.

Although the Disciples have a great deal of experience when it comes to catching fish, they follow the words of Jesus and throw out their nets once again. And indeed, they are hardly able to gather them in again, so full of fishes are they. "That disciple whom Jesus loved said to Peter, 'It is the Lord!'" (Jn 21:7) Since following Jesus' words led to a successful catch, the Beloved Disciple realises that it is the Lord himself standing on the shore and talking to them. But do we only experience Resurrection when our lives turn out well, when we are successful? Does this mean that those who are not successful, cannot experience the Resurrection? John's aim in his Resurrection stories is to encourage those, in particular, who suffer from a sense of futility and for whom the night has fallen. For them, too, Resurrection is possible. They, too, will one day gather in nets full of fishes. Then they will confess together with the Beloved Disciple: "It is the Lord!"

My life does not have to be going well for me to make the confession of the Beloved Disciple. For me Easter means that I say to myself, "It is the Lord", particularly in the kind of situations when I sit at my desk and do not know how to resolve my problems at work, or when I sit through a fruitless meeting. When I bring this word with me, into all the situations of my life, then the grey morning becomes transfigured. Then the veil of futility, which had covered everything, is removed: the Resurrection happens for me. When I can believe that the Risen One is where I am, where I toil, all too often without success, then my heart will expand. I get an insight how, even in my failure and futility, I am able to experience the Resurrection.

Try to say to yourself today, in all that you do and that you encounter, "It is the Lord". When you go for a walk, say to yourself, "It is the Lord". When you are at work and have a problem with your colleagues, hold these words before your eyes! And perhaps the desolate grey of your life will be transfigured, and you will recognise the Lord standing on the shore of your life, the Lord who steps into your life from another world, in order to transfigure it. You will look at your life with fresh eyes and perceive the presence of the Risen One in everything. And your torn-ness and hopelessness, your futility and resignation will be healed.

• TUESDAY •

Transformation of our lives

(John 21:7-11)

On hearing the Beloved Disciple's words, Peter immediately plunges into the lake. But before so doing, he puts his outer garment on again. This might not seem to be very sensible. It means that he will face Jesus with wet clothes. Obviously Peter is so enthused when he hears that it is Jesus, that he jumps immediately into the water, in order to be the first to reach Jesus. For an Oriental, Biblical exegetes tell us, decency would demand that one appear in front of another person fully dressed. Perhaps, though, Peter's action has a symbolic meaning. The outer garment is a symbol of the roles we play and of the masks we wear. And water symbolises the Subconscious. If we want to appear before the Risen One, the upper garment must first be immersed in the water of the unconscious, so that our real shape becomes more apparent through the masks and roles we assume. When it comes to an encounter with the Risen One, an external appearance of self-assurance is of no use: we must come as people who have been soaked through and through, as people who are no longer frozen, no longer held by the rigidity of the grave, whose every part has come into contact with the water of life.

The other disciples come to the shore with the boat and the net, where they see a charcoal fire on the ground and on it, fish. Next to the fish is some bread. Jesus already has the fish for which he asked them at the beginning of the scene. He asks the disciples to bring some of their fishes as well. All this does not appear to be very logical. But John is not concerned with logic, but with mystery: which in fact becomes clear in the number that he suddenly quotes. When Peter pulled the net ashore, it was filled with 153 large fishes. Biblical exegetes have scratched their heads over this number. Augustine explained the number thus: if you add all the numbers to each other, from one to seventeen, the result is 153. One is the figure of wholeness, seven that of transformation. Through the Resurrection, then, our life is transformed and becomes both whole and healed.

I have long been fascinated by the interpretation given by Evagrios Pontikos (b. 399). He subdivided his book *On Prayer* into 153 small chapters. In his introduction he states the reason for this: "I have divided this discourse on prayer into one hundred and fifty-three texts. In this way I send you an evangelical feast, so that you may delight in a symbolical number that combines a triangular with a hexagonal figure. The triangle indicates spiritual knowledge of the Trinity, the hexagon indicates the ordered creation of the world in six days. The number one hundred is square, while the number fifty-three is triangular and spherical; for twenty-eight is triangular, and twenty-five is spherical, five times five being twenty-five. In this way, you have a square figure to express the fourfold nature of the virtues, and also a spherical number, twenty-five, which by form represents the cyclic movement of time and so indicates true knowledge of this present age... The triangle can signify knowledge of the

Holy Trinity". (Evagrios Pontikos) Evagrios' interpretation is a little complicated. But it shows that for him the mystery of the Resurrection comes to fulfilment in contemplation. In contemplation we begin to understand the world in a new way. Through it we see God in all things. Resurrection, according to this numerical symbolism, means that God and the world become the same, that we can experience God through earthly things. And Resurrection means that we become one with the threefold God. When Resurrection happens to us, all opposites within us are united, the square, circle and triangle fall together. All that is square, that has edges, becomes round. In the Resurrection we are lifted above ourselves, together with all our inner contraries, into unity with God. In God everything that is at odds within us, becomes one. Thus for Evagrios the Resurrection is the fulfilment of our self-becoming. We come, in God, to our true selves.

Evagrios invites you today to ponder on all the vexed contraries of your life and to trust that they will not tear you apart, but that they will become one in the encounter with the Risen One. You do not have to dissolve the inner tension that at times threatens to tear you apart. You need only hold it out to God. If you hold it out to God in prayer, without judging it, then you will experience the acceptance of God in your dividedness. This will give you a deep inner peace amid the contradictions you experience, a foretaste of the healing, completion and wholeness that is to come. Such, for Evagrios, is the experience of the Resurrection.

• WEDNESDAY •

Jesus in our midst

(John 21:12-14)

Jesus breaks his fast with the disciples in an odd atmosphere: "Jesus said to them, 'Come and have breakfast.' Now none of the disciples dared to ask him, 'Who are you?' because they knew it was the Lord." (Jn 21:12) Jesus himself invites the disciples to the meal. He talks to them. But there is no dialogue. You can tell from the brief description given by John that the disciples really want to ask: Who are you? But no one dares. No one has the courage to address Jesus and talk to him. The atmosphere is one of awe and bewilderment, but also of silent joy. All present sense a mystery that cannot be explained. Words would only serve to make it trite. The disciples experience the transformation of their grey morning, the sudden creation of an atmosphere of love and intimacy. Their hearts are touched, mysteriously moved.

John describes the meal in a few words: "Jesus came and took the bread and gave it to them, and did the same with the fish." (Jn 21:13) The scene he describes is a Eucharistic one, and the words he uses are the same as those used to describe the multiplication of the loaves. (cf. Jn 6:11). However, the word 'eucharistesas', 'he gave thanks', is missing. Some exegetes think that this is proof that the early meal by Lake Tiberias is not to be understood eucharistically. But for me the absence of these words means something else. The multiplication of the loaves was the promise of the Eucharist. After it, Jesus gave his important discourse on the Bread of Life, in which he explained the mystery of the Eucharist to the disciples. Now, after his Resurrection, he holds the Eucharist himself with the disciples. Instead of the words 'gave thanks' the text has 'erchetai', 'he comes, steps forward'. In the Eucharist the Risen One steps into our midst, he comes to us from the other shore in order to hold a meal with us. Heaven and earth join each other. The disciples who step out of the boat in which they have laboured in vain the whole night, are an image of ourselves: we emerge from the night of our life, in which we often drift aimlessly along on the sea, often shaken to and fro by the wind and the waves. But Jesus comes to us and he has a meal with us. Then our lives are transformed. Resurrection happens to us and in us.

Jesus gives the disciples loaves and fishes: the bread of heaven mentioned by Jesus in his Eucharistic speech: "I am the living bread that came down from heaven. Whoever eats of this bread will live forever" (Jn 6:51). Fish is an image of immortality. The Early Church saw the fish as the symbol of Christ, not only because the letters of the Greek word, ICHTYS, contain the first letters of the Greek phrase 'Jesus Christ, Son of God, Saviour', but also because the image of a fish was used to represent Christ himself. In Antiquity fish was the food of the dead and the symbol of life and happiness. Augustine sees the baked fish as an image of Christ who has suffered for us: "piscis assus Christus est passus". In the Early Church the fish was a highly popular Eucharistic symbol. In the

Eucharist Christ, who has died for us and is risen for us, gives us the food of immortality. In the Eucharist he plants the divine seed of immortality into our transient nature and thus takes us up into his immortal divinity.

If we read our Eucharistic feasts in the light of the breakfast by Lake Tiberias, we see how in each Eucharist Jesus steps in our midst from the other shore. He transforms the grey futility of our life into an atmosphere of intimacy and love. The Risen One himself comes towards us in each Eucharist. He invites us to "Come and eat". We eat the bread that comes from heaven, in order to satisfy our deepest hunger; we eat the living bread that fills us with the sense of aliveness for which we all long. And in his blood we drink the drink of immortality, represented in the symbol of the fish, the drink which makes us immortal ourselves.

When you take part in the Eucharistic feast, imagine the intimate and loving atmosphere that characterised the breakfast by Lake Tiberias. Imagine that the Risen One steps into this motley community from the shore of eternity, that he gazes lovingly into the disappointed and sad faces and holds out to everybody the bread of life and the wine of love, so that they might experience Resurrection: that they may be enlightened, be raised up and rise in order to greet the true life, life in God.

The question of our love

(John 21:15-17)

The Greeks have three words for love: 'eros', 'philia' and 'agape'. Eros is the passionate, possessive form of love; philia, the love between friends; and agape, pure love, which both human beings and God share. All three types of love are connected. Some biblical exegetes think that agape is far superior to eros. But if this were the case, then divine love would be a bloodless love. Divine love, too, must needs be soaked in the passion of eros so that it can transform our lives. In the same way philia needs eros and agape: only then does a friend know himself or herself to be fully accepted and loved. Every person has a deep longing to be loved and to love. Yet our longing is often disappointed. We know through experience that love can enchant us and break through the walls of our defence mechanisms. At the same time, we all too often experience our love as fragile, as riddled with possessiveness, with an urge for power and with all kinds of fears. John's Gospel aims to show us how Jesus makes people who have become alienated from themselves and incapable of loving, able to love once again. To this end, John concludes his three Resurrection encounters by looking at the question of love.

The threefold question that Jesus addresses to Peter is not principally concerned with the high degree of love required in one who leads the

Church, but with the question of how we can learn genuine and authentic love. Jesus repeats this question to Peter three times, a reference to his threefold denial. If we talk about our loving, we must always do it in the knowledge that we have all too often betrayed love, that despite all our longing for love, we have time and time again turned away from it. We cannot pretend that we are wonderful lovers of God and humankind. We need modesty and caution when we talk about our loving. We should not be too quick to talk of it; we should rather talk carefully and attentively about our attempts to love genuinely and fully.

When Jesus asks Peter if he loves him, the Greek text uses the word 'agape' the first two times: he is asking Peter whether he loves him with a love that is free from ego, from the intention to possess the other for oneself. And Peter replies both times, "Lord, you know that I love you (*philo se*)." Peter can claim to love Jesus as a friend, with a love that is full of feeling, that takes pleasure in his company and rejoices in him. At the same time, his response to Jesus means: "Lord, you know it. You can sense that I love you. It is not just my imagination. My love for my friend is true. Our friendship is true. I sense the same feelings in you." In his third question Jesus changes the word. Now he is asking, "Phileis me – do you love me as a friend?" Peter is saddened. Perhaps he is sad because he remembers his betrayal.

Or perhaps he is sad because Jesus questions his friendship. A friendship which, to Peter, is clear. He never dared assert that he loves Jesus with completely selfless love (agape); but he never doubted his feelings of love and friendship. Now Jesus even questions his feelings. He should, says Jesus, look at them more closely, to see whether they really are what he thinks they are. To what extent have other motives become mixed up with his feelings? Is it not something special to be a friend of Jesus? Hasn't Peter made use of his big friend for his own ends and to boost his feeling of self-worth? Is it really the love of a friend, which rejoices in the other, which lets the other be as they are? Or does Peter only really want to put the other Disciples in the shade, so that he can boast of being Jesus' best friend? Peter replies to this question: "Lord, you know everything; you know that I love you (philo se)." (Jn 21:17) Peter opens his heart to Jesus and lets him look inside. He wants to tell him: "Lord, you see through my heart. You know how much egoism is in my love, how much calculation, how much possessiveness and jealousy. But you also know that in spite of it all, something in my love is entirely pure, that in the depths of my heart it is you I want; that I want to love you truly; that there is in me at least the longing for this pure love".

Think about the love you have, your love for your friend, for your spouse, your children, your colleagues, and your love for God, for Christ! Hold your heart out to God and let him study and examine it! Repeat to yourself the question which Jesus used three times to awaken Peter from some of his complacency! Hold out to God everything that is calculating and impure! Trust that in you, too, lives pure love, that you really do want to love other people just as they are, that in you there is a deep longing to love God with all your heart. Even if you do not often feel love for God, even if pure love seems a very distant reality, there is within you at least an intuitive grasp of, and a genuine longing for, this love – a love which makes your life truly worth living. Trust your longing! Trust your love! Then you will experience Resurrection today.

• FRIDAY •

What does it matter to you?

(John 21:18-23)

The conversation between Peter and Jesus in John's Gospel, which follows on from the quizzing of Peter, is an odd one. Jesus does not reward Peter for loving him, but he believes him capable of, and entrusts him with, a destiny that is similar to his own. He believes him capable of going to his death for love of him, of being prepared to give himself into the hands of God, not knowing where they will lead him. Peter is obviously prepared to die for Jesus, to be nailed to the cross as his beloved master was. With his words, "Follow me" (Jn 21:19), Jesus bids Peter to follow him into martyrdom. Peter says yes to his violent death. But when he sees the Beloved Disciple follow Jesus, he wants to know exactly what will happen to him. This question is rebuffed curtly: "what does it matter to you?" (Jn 21:22) The path of every single person is a mystery. It is not for Peter to know the destiny of the others. He is asked to follow Jesus not because everyone else does it, but because he loves him. Love does not compare. It does not depend on the behaviour of others. It loves because it loves.

Resurrection does not mean that we can now stride out and go wherever we please. Resurrection proves itself if we are prepared to let ourselves be girded by God and led by him to a place where we do not want to go. Faith in the Resurrection frees us from desperately clinging on to our lives and from being fixated on the path we are trying to follow at any cost. The love which Peter confessed to the Risen One follows the beloved wherever they may go: what really counts is being with the beloved, in life or in death, in joy or in suffering, in freedom or in the ties that bind. Peter still has to learn about this love. I understand why he compares himself with John, the Beloved Disciple. When many of my brothers left religious life in the early 1970s, I asked myself whether I was only staying because this or that brother was himself still holding on. We would like to follow Jesus, but we want to stipulate our own terms. Only if those who we love go the same way, are we prepared to follow Jesus everywhere. Only because my brother meditates daily, do I remain on the inner path. Only because my friend takes part in the citizens' initiative, do I take part too, even though many things about it annoy me. Left to myself, I would have given up a long time ago. Jesus challenges not only Peter, but also every single one of us to follow our own personal path, without glancing to the left or the to right to see whether the others are doing the same. Love looks only at the beloved and not at how I am doing in comparison with the others. Go through today keeping the words of Jesus present: "What does it matter to you?" Observe closely those areas in which you compare yourself with others, where you feel you may have been short-changed or that you are better than the others! How often do you think about others, do you think about their destiny? "What does it matter to you?" Keep returning your thoughts to yourself and go on your way. These words of Jesus will become a 'koan'[1], unlocking the mystery of your life for you. When you decide to end the continual comparison of self to others, you will become one with yourself, in harmony with your path. Only then will you become able to walk every step with the care it requires. And every step will lead you to life and to love. You go because you go. You go because you love. You go your own path, which leads you into your own unique 'gestalt' – the unique way in which you alone can give expression to God on this earth.

• SATURDAY •

The open heart

(Acts 10:9-48)

In the Acts of the Apostles Luke recounts how Peter gives witness before the people to the love that has revealed itself in Jesus Christ. It is a Resurrection narrative: Peter suddenly throws the legalistic principles of his earlier thinking overboard;

his heart widens and he proclaims the Good News of Jesus' death and Resurrection to the pagans as well. In John's Gospel Jesus initiates Peter into his leadership office. Peter can lead the Church only if he loves Jesus. In the Acts of the Apostles God sends his angel to Peter and shows him in a vision how he should live this love. He is to give it to all people. He is to deprive no one of the message of the Resurrection, and he is not to refuse baptism to anyone who believes in Jesus. But the angel not only challenges Peter to love, he also enables him to do so. He widens his heart through a dream. In the dream Peter's narrow thought structures are prised open and new thoughts are coaxed out of him.

God sends an angel to the pious Roman centurion Cornelius; the angel commands him to send a few men to Joppe to a certain Simon. The next day, Peter has a vision around midday, when he is at prayer. He sees heaven open, and a large linen cloth come down, covered with all kinds of quadrupeds, reptiles and birds. The dietary laws of the Jewish people would not allow them to eat the meat of these animals. But a voice calls out to Peter: "Get up, Peter; kill and eat." (Acts 10:13) Peter resists. Still the voice persists: "What God has made clean, you must not call profane." (Acts 10:15) While Peter is still reflecting on the vision, the men from Joppe arrive and ask for him. Peter goes with them to Cornelius and speaks to him and his relatives and friends, proclaiming the news of Jesus Christ in such a way that Romans and Greeks can understand it. He talks about Jesus in the language and way of thinking typical of the Greeks, "how he went about doing good and healing all who were oppressed by the devil, for God was with him." (Acts 10:38) Although Jesus did good, he was killed: "but God raised him on the third day and allowed him to appear, not to all the people but to us who were chosen by God as witnesses" (Acts 10:40f). While Peter is still preaching, the Holy Spirit comes down on all. To the Jewish mind such a miracle is impossible: the Holy Spirit poured down on the Gentiles. Peter gives the order to have all baptised in the name of Jesus Christ and explains the decision by saying: "Can anyone withhold the water for baptising these people who have received the Holy Spirit just as we have?" (Acts 10:47)

For Luke the Resurrection is clearly at work when people who are caught up in narrow legalistic thinking – such as tends to blight us all – unexpectedly get a large heart and offer God's grace to all people. Peter would probably never have left the restricting framework of the beliefs he held previously of his own accord: God himself led him to this breadth through a vision, through an angel. In such inner images, in dreams and visions and in the encounter with the angel we too can experience the Resurrection, can awaken to new opportunities and ways of behaving, and the widening of our hearts.

Perhaps you have had dreams which have increased your inner breadth and enabled you to act in new ways. Suddenly you were able to approach a person with whom you previously wanted nothing to do. Suddenly you were able to tackle a task which you had previously always avoided. Think about those places in your life where you have already experienced the Resurrection, where you were able to let go of narrow legalistic thinking, where you shed your inhibitions, where you dealt with your passions free from fear, where you let go of your old patterns of thought and behaviour! Trust that God will send you his angel again and again, so that your heart may increase in breadth and your love stream forth from an open heart into everything that you encounter – into the people you meet, but also into the things in your room and to the flowers in your garden! Breathe in, let the love of God stream into your heart, and imagine how this process fills it with oxygen and how everything around you is touched by the love of God.

1. A form of Buddhism meditation, in which a problem which admits of no solution is proposed.

Resurrection and Ascension

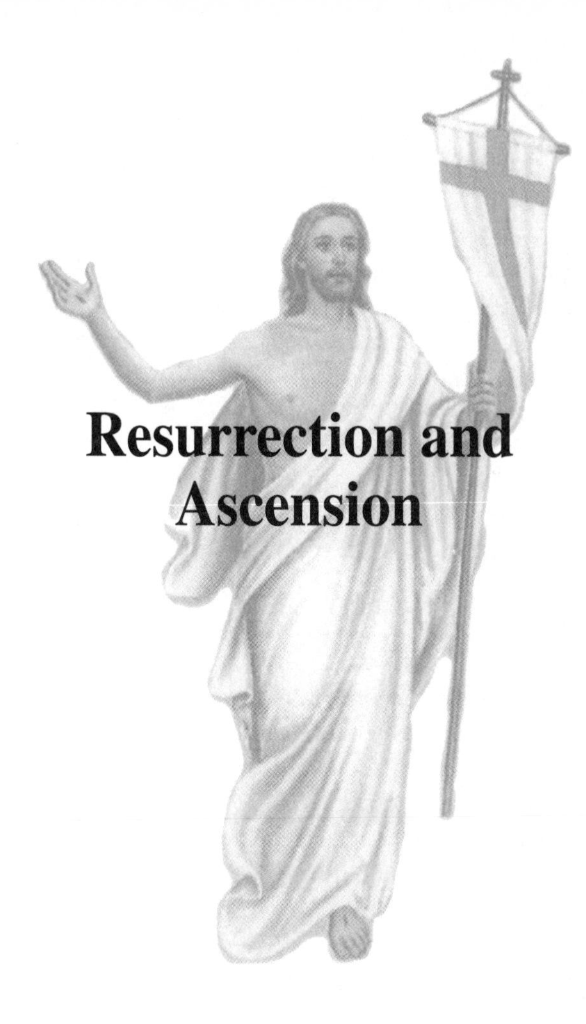

SIXTH WEEK OF EASTER

Farewell and consolation

(John 14:18-20)

The feast of the Ascension of Christ is celebrated in the sixth week of Easter. The Gospels on all days of this week are taken from the farewell discourses at the Last Supper. In them Jesus consoles his Disciples by saying that he will not leave them alone when he goes to his death or, as the liturgy understands these words, if he now ascends into heaven: "I will not leave you orphaned; I am coming to you." (Jn 14:18) Even though Jesus now goes to the Father, he will not leave us behind as orphans. Although he is no longer with us, as he was with the Disciples, when he could be touched, heard, seen, he is nevertheless with us in a different way. We need the eyes of faith, in order to recognise his presence in us and among us: "In a little while the world will no longer see me, but you will see me; because I live, you also will live. On that day you will know that I am in my Father, and you in me, and I in you." (Jn 14:19f) The world is unable to see the Risen One. The believer, however, sees Jesus. The believer knows that Jesus is alive. This is for me an important hallmark of the true experience of God – where I live and where life blossoms in me, there I see the Risen One and there I experience God. In our aliveness, which rises from the rigidity of the grave, which blossoms out of our emptiness, we recognise the Risen One.

In the life which conquers death within us, we

will recognise that Christ is in the Father and that we are in Christ and Christ in us. Such is the message of consolation which he has left us at his departure. He no longer walks by our side, but he will be in us, and we will be in him. The Ascension creates a new closeness to Christ. Although we cannot see and hear Christ externally, he is in us, he has become our innermost self. There we can hear him in the silent motions of our hearts. There we can see him when we gaze inside ourselves and perceive a deep inner peace at the bottom of our soul. Evagrios Pontikos, the most important monastic writer of the fourth century, calls the inner room within us, in which Christ himself lives, 'show of peace'. We cannot see Christ in his external form, but we see him with the eyes of faith as peace, as harmony and being at one with ourselves. This peace is visible: its presence is revealed by a certain charisma that a person seems to possess, by the harmony of their movements, by the radiance that comes from their faces, by the way in which their words are in tune with their being.

Jesus knows that his Disciples are full of sadness. But he promises us that our sorrow will be transformed into joy. He compares us with the woman who is afflicted when her time to give birth draws near: "But when her child is born, she no longer remembers the anguish because of the joy of having brought a human being into the world. So you have pain now; but I will see you again, and your hearts will rejoice, and no one will take your joy from you." (Jn 16:21f) Because Jesus goes to the Father through his death and his ascension into heaven, we can experience a new birth, we are, so to speak, born as a new person. How are we to understand this? We shed our old identity, which we had used to define ourselves before the world: liberating ourselves from success and failure, recognition and affection. By shedding our old identity, our being is determined by the fact that Christ is in us. Since we are in Christ true joy is now within us, a joy that no one can take away. Christ identifies himself not only with love, but also with joy (cf. Jn 15:10f). In him we get in touch with the true love and true joy which are waiting for us in the depths of our souls, but which are all too often without connection to our conscious being.

Jesus' farewell to the Disciples reminds us of all the farewells we ourselves have had to make. You have had to bid farewell to your childhood, your youth, to the times when you enjoyed success, when you were needed, when you were at the centre, when you were full of strength; when you took your leave of dear people, of places where life was a pleasure. Every leave-taking hurts. But every farewell is also a new start. Think of the things you are called to leave behind today! What things would you like to leave behind you, so that new life can blossom within you? When you go for a walk, imagine how with every step you leave behind people, places, habits, injuries, disappointments, in order to stride out, deliberately, and cover new ground. You are able to say farewell because you have the consolation of knowing that you will not be going on your journey on your own, that the Risen One goes with you and is in you.

• MONDAY •

Heaven opens over your depths

(Luke 24:50f)

Luke describes the Ascension of Jesus into heaven in a few concise words: "lifting up his hands, he blessed them. While he was blessing them, he withdrew from them and was carried up into heaven." (Lk 24:50f) Jesus' Ascension causes heaven to open up over us. The Early Christians used to raise their hands to God in prayer. They prayed in the 'orante' posture[1]. If I pray with my hands raised, I can imagine that my prayer causes heaven to open over my life. Deeply rooted in the earth I lift my hands to heaven. Heaven then extends right into the darkness of my fear, into the earthliness and instinctiveness of my life. And in prayer I open heaven not just over myself, but over the people who are close to my heart, even over the town where I happen to be, over the entire country. When many people pray together with raised hands, one can well imagine that heaven opens for all for whom it had previously been closed and clouded, for those who no longer have a sense of God, or time for him, who no longer direct their gaze heavenwards but who are only concerned with getting along here on earth. In prayer, heaven opens above us and above our world. This became clear to me when I took part in the service for the Feast of the Transfiguration on Mount Athos, which lasted a whole night. In the darkness of the night a window was thrust open, and we could look up into heaven. When we sing psalms and songs for hours on end, we see the whole world in a new light. The world is no longer closed, it is open to heaven, and heaven and earth touch each other at the place where we are praying.

In John's Gospel Jesus said, "No one has ascended into heaven except the one who descended from heaven, the Son of Man." (Jn 3:13) Celebrating the Ascension of Christ does not mean that we flee from this earth to heaven, that we, the heavenly-minded, leave the earth far behind. Pious people are often in danger of becoming so fascinated by God that they would prefer to leave everything that is of this earth behind. But the myth of Icarus, who would leave the earth behind and fell to his death, shows how impossible this course is. We can never forget that we are creatures of the earth, instinctive, and have our share of darkness within. Only if we have the courage to descend into our humanity, will heaven open above us. This Saint Benedict demonstrates in his chapter on humility, in which he sees Jacob's ladder as an image of our spiritual path: only those who descend to the earth, to the humus ('humilitas', 'humility' as the return to the earth) are able to ascend into heaven. Luke writes in his Gospel that heaven opens over Jesus at precisely the moment he descends into the water of the river Jordan, into the floods that were made murky by the sin of the whole of humanity, into the water of the unconscious, into the shadowlands inhabited by the demons, the powers of this earth. Precisely at the place where Jesus comes into contact with that which poses the greatest threat to humanity, heaven was opened above him (Lk 3:21f). And when Jesus, filled with fear, prayed on the Mount of Olives to be 'spared' the 'cup' of a violent death, when his cold sweat fell onto the ground like drops of blood, when he felt that his Disciples had abandoned him, heaven was opened above him once again, and an angel came down and strengthened him (Lk 22:43f). When we are at our wits' end, when we do not know how to go on, when we are full of fear and doubt in spite of our faith, heaven is opened above us. God sends his angel to strengthen us. The angel connects heaven and earth. He brings heaven to earth, into our fear and misery.

In which areas of your life do you seek to escape the earth and its narrowness? Do you use heaven as an escape from the difficulties that assail you? Or have you experienced heaven opening up above your fear? What does 'ascent through descent' mean to you? In which areas of your life do you refuse to descend into the depths of your inner abyss? Meditate on the two scenes of the Baptism of Jesus (Lk 3:21f) and the prayer of Jesus on the Mount of Olives (Lk 22:43f)! May heaven be opened above your fear and above the sinful waters of your own life.

• TUESDAY •

Heaven is within you

(Acts 1:10f)

But it is not sufficient to seek for heaven above us. In the Acts of the Apostles Luke tells us that the Disciples keep looking heavenward in order to watch Jesus ascending. Then "suddenly two men in white robes stood by them. They said, 'Men of Galilee, why do you stand looking up toward heaven?'" (Acts 1:10f) The two angels inform the men that Jesus will come again, and so instead of watching his departure, they should watch out for his return. Jesus is now to be found in their own hearts. Angelus Silesius gave this thought a classical expression in his well-known verse from the 'Cherubinic Wanderer':

> Stop, where are you going? Heaven is
> inside you.
> Look for God elsewhere, and you will
> miss him time and time again.

Heaven is not to be found anywhere else but within ourselves. This accords with Luke's vision of the world. Luke was a Greek. He describes Jesus as the divine wanderer who descended from heaven to remind us of our divine core, and to remind us that the Kingdom of God is within us, that heaven is within us. We are not only people of this earth, but also people of heaven. In Jesus, God has visited us. Luke is here thinking of those Greek Myths in which the gods appear to people in human form. In Zechariah's prophesy and song of praise we read: "Blessed be the Lord, the God of Israel / He has visited his people and redeemed them... The loving-kindness of the heart of our God / Who visits us like the dawn from on high" (Lk 1:68.78). In Jesus, God himself comes down to earth and visits us. He comes to visit us in our home: the home of our communities, but also the inner house of our heart, in order that we might taste God's charity and love of humankind.

Origen, the great Greek theologian, gave the same thought expression, phrased in Latin, with the following words: 'Coelum es et in coelum ibis', 'You are heaven and you go to heaven'. We are people who both carry heaven within ourselves and who are on the way to heaven. Both of these ideas are central to Luke's Gospel. We are, like Jesus, wanderers between heaven and earth. Like Jesus, we are journeying towards heaven. Augustine expressed this experience in the following words: 'Portando Deum coeli, coelum sumus', 'In carrying the God of heaven, we are heaven'. Heaven is already in us, as Christ is in us. But at the same time, we are on the path to heaven, where we will see Christ in his glory. In answer to the question 'Where is God hiding?', a Hassidic story replies, 'In the human heart'. God dwells in the human heart. And where God dwells, there is heaven.

Of all monastic writers, Evagrios Pontikos speaks insistently of the inner space that is inside every person. For him it is the space of love and the space which is free from the murkiness resulting from the passions. Evagrios uses different images to describe this space. It is the place of God. Within this space sparkles a light like sapphire. It is Jerusalem, show of peace. In that space we are at one with ourselves. From the monks of the Middle Ages we have the comparison, 'cella est coelum', 'the cell is heaven'. By this they do not just mean the monk's physical cell, where the monk is alone with his God and communes with his God in friendship, but the cell as an inner place, the space of pure silence, in which God dwells in us. This space is the heaven in which the monk lives together with God. The monks also refer to this space as the 'valetuninarium', 'the infirmary, the place of recovery'. If we regularly lock ourselves in this inner room in prayer, we can be healed of our hurts and wounds and gain fresh strength. In this inner cell God's healing and loving presence envelops us.

Try meditating using one of the images mentioned above. Imagine that heaven is within you and that you carry God in the heaven within! Or sit down peacefully in your room! Look around at what you perceive in the room where you spend so many hours a day! And then imagine that your room is the place where God lives with you, where God wants to commune with you, where God heals your wounds!

• WEDNESDAY •

The inner master

(Luke 24:51)

Jesus bids farewell to the Disciples and leaves them. They are now no longer able to follow him in a physical sense. Jesus is not a guru whom one follows. He has ascended into heaven in order to be close to us in a new way. He has become our inner master. But when does someone really come close to us? They are close to us when we touch them, talk to them, kiss them. But in this closeness there is always also a distance. Sometimes we do not feel the other person at all. Even in touch we often remain on the surface and do not reach the heart of the other person. Jesus is no longer with us in a physical sense; we cannot touch him, feel him or take hold of him. So that he can ascend into heaven we must let go of him. We must take our leave of the illusions that we have created about our life. We must take our leave of all that we depend on, all that we are attached to, but also of the burden of the past, of the hurts and wounds that mark our life story. We cannot carry them around with us forever – if we do so we will remain earth-bound, and we cannot be lifted up into heaven with Jesus.

Many people today are addicted to following a guru. Some style themselves as gurus, others are turned into one by their followers. Jesus is no guru. He ascended into heaven so that we do not imitate him externally, but come rather to resemble him internally. Paul talks about putting on Christ like a garment. We can become one with him by identifying not with his mind alone, but with his innermost being, his spirit, with all that constitutes him. Following Jesus does not mean denying our own way of thinking and feeling. We follow Jesus when we enter into harmony with our inner self, when we follow the inner master. The inner master talks to us through our thoughts and feelings, through our dreams, through our body, through the many inner impulses that he provides each day – if only we listen attentively enough.

Having Jesus as our inner master does not mean that he has become our super-ego, that we have internalised his principles in the same way as we did the messages of our parents. The inner master requires permanent confrontation. We should confront everything that emerges within us with Jesus and ask if it truly comes from him. Some say, in all that I do I should ask myself: 'What would Jesus say to this?' That can often be helpful, but we must beware of putting the voice of our own super-ego into Jesus' mouth. In order to recognise what Jesus would say, we must listen to our innermost voice. But then there is the danger of our confusing our own notions and ideas with those of Jesus. What we need, time and time again, is to confront our own thoughts and feelings with the words which Jesus said. In doing so, we must not try to understand the words of Jesus by the letter; rather, we must meditate on them and so enter into them, in order to discover the Spirit of Jesus in them: "Now the Lord is the Spirit, and where the Spirit of the Lord is, there is freedom." (2 Cor 3:17)

Do you know your inner master? Or do you prefer to follow external masters, letting yourself be guided by them because the path seems safer that way? Trust that Christ as the inner master will show you, from the depths of your heart, the path that you are to go! In your heart you will find all you need to live well. Do not make yourself dependent on the opinions of others! Do not look incessantly for others to show you the right way to live! Your inner master will guide you along the way, and you will grow ever more into the unique and incomparable image of yourself which God has created. When you listen attentively inside yourself, you know very well, deep down, what is truly good for you, what will help you advance further along your inner way. But you need to trust this inner master. We keep wanting to make sure, by looking to others to confirm that our path is the right one. You must do without this confirmation and trust the inner master. He will lead you on your path better than any spiritual or therapeutic companion could.

• THURSDAY •

Lifted up, beyond and above ourselves

(Psalms 68:19)

When Jesus was lifted into heaven, he took his human nature with him to the Father. But in his humanity he took us into heaven with him: our vitality and sexuality, our fears, our longings, our needs and passions, our strength and our weakness. The liturgy expresses this mystery in the curious psalm verse sung at today's feast for the Alleluia: "The Lord came from Sinai into the holy place. Ascending on high, he led captivity captive" (ascendens captivam duxit captivitatem, Ps 68:17f; 67:18f). This psalm verse is difficult to translate. Jerome interpreted it as meaning that Christ, in ascending into heaven, carried the captives with him, captive. Or are Jerome's words to be translated as meaning that Christ took captivity captive, i.e. that he released us from our captivity? Whatever the answer, the liturgy understands these enigmatic words as a description of Jesus' ascension into heaven.

The liturgy obviously understands the Ascension of Christ as meaning that Christ will take humanity, which is trapped within itself or shackled by Satan, into heaven with him. We frequently have the experience of being entrapped here on earth, imprisoned by our fear and sadness. We cannot get away from ourselves, enmeshed in the ebb and flow of our emotions, needs and passions, in our guilt and feelings of guilt. We are caught in ambiguous relationships, in intrigues and role-plays. We are stuck within ourselves, within our pride which does not allow us to see ourselves as we really are. We are bound to our body, which all too often holds us in a tight grip. In his Ascension to heaven Jesus laid his hand on us, he caught us with his love. And thus he has transformed our prison. He has taken us into heaven in his love. As Karl Rahner put it, "He has taken with him that which he had taken on. The infirm flesh and the human spirit, which was darkened in the suffering of death and was at a loss for answers, and the trembling heart. That which I am: this narrow hole, full of darkness, in which questions and all the 'not understood' is lurking around like squeaking rats and finds no way out" (Rahner). Our prison, our darkness, our coldness, our loneliness, our alienation: through Christ's Ascension all these have been lifted up into the area of God, into heaven, into the space of divine love. There we are kept safe, lifted up, beyond and above ourselves. There we are already at home.

The Feast of Christ's Ascension draws our attention to a new image of humanity. In lifting our human nature up into heaven, Christ has given it a divine dignity, and shown us that only if we are capable of taking a step beyond our nature – into heaven where Jesus ascended in body and spirit, with heart and soul – can we become truly human. We are human, but that is not the end of the story. When we become fixated on our humanity alone, we make our life down here on earth hell. We can only live truly human lives if we allow ourselves to be lifted beyond ourselves, into the divine space. Only in God does our human-ness come to its fulfilment.

No Feast of the Ascension of Christ could be complete if I failed to take a walk along the Bachallee, a path alongside a brook in our monastery, with the Alleluia verse ('captivam duxit captivitatem', 'He led captivity captive') for company. I imagine myself walking along the alleyway as I am, with all my dependencies, my captivity, my ties, my unfreedom, but that at the same time I am lifted beyond myself in Christ, taken with him into heaven. Try to meditate on the Alleluia verse as you go about your tasks today: it may help you to open up the mystery of your humanity; you will be lifted out of your imprisonment, lifted up into heaven in spite of being earth-bound.

In another of my rituals I repeat to myself the words of St Paul from the same feast: "Our place of citizenship is in heaven" (Phil 3:20). Sometimes I do the same with the question asked by Novalis: 'Where do we go, then? – We always return home'. And so an awareness begins to grow within me, that I will always be on a journey until I reach my lasting home, heaven. Only there will my journey end.

• FRIDAY •

Easter joy in everyday life

(Luke 4:52f)

The Disciples "returned to Jerusalem with great joy; and they were continually in the temple blessing God" (Lk 24:52f). With these words the Gospel of Luke concludes. The Disciples do not remain rooted to the spot where Jesus took his leave from them, fascinated. They go home, but have changed: now they are filled with great joy. And this joy enables them to change the way they live and work. The experience of the Ascension sends us back into our everyday lives, where we live and work. Our task is to bring heaven into the everyday, where hell is, where emptiness and meaninglessness prevail. Joy expands the heart and opens us up for the encounter with others; it enlivens us so that we can go about our work with joy and creativity. Those who live their everyday life in this joy, open up heaven over all those who they meet.

The Scriptures tell us that the Disciples were always in the Temple, praising God. In divine worship, in the communal praising of God, the Disciples experienced the heaven into which Jesus was taken up: it opened up a window to heaven for them. The experience of the Ascension led them back into the temple time and again. For us, too, worship could well be the place where we see heaven open up. Of course there are services that drag on and are tiresome and boring. There are times, however, when we experience a certain 'dense' quality in the atmosphere during the singing, listening and the Eucharistic meal: and heaven opens up. During our liturgy, the Church tells us, we take part in the divine liturgy celebrated by the angels and saints before the face of God. When I become aware during the Divine Office that "before the angels I sing your praise" (Ps 138:1, RB 19:5), I find that everything else is put into perspective. I do not escape from the problems of my everyday life, but I sense that they lose their impact, that they no longer burden me. Still there, they do not dominate me: I feel free. Then heaven is truly opened. And heaven, open, also opens my heart and widens it: my heart can now feel joy. A closed heart cannot experience joy. Joy comes into being only when the heart widens.

You cannot force yourself to be joyful. The mere fact of my calling you to be joyful will hardly make you feel full of joy. But when you call to mind the images of Easter and the Ascension and meditate on them, your heart may well widen and be filled with joy. The joy is already inside you. You do not have to create it artificially. All too often you are cut off from this joy, because you worry too much about all that is not good inside yourself and around you. Allow yourself to be brought into touch with your joy through Easter and the Ascension! And try to look at your life under the wide horizon of heaven with a wide heart! Then you will discover the joy that lies ready at the bottom of your heart. The joy of Easter will transform your everyday life. You will find it easier to fulfil your tasks.

We are of God's kind

(Acts 17:29)

When I look in the Acts of the Apostles for a narrative that describes the mystery of the Ascension of Christ most accurately, I think of the sermon that Paul gave on the Areopagus in Athens. It is probably the most discussed speech in world literature. On the Areopagus the Athenians liked to discuss the many philosophical currents that existed at the time. Paul begins his sermon by calling the Athenians particularly God-fearing. He says that among the objects of their worship he found an altar bearing the inscription, "To an unknown God" (Acts 17:23). Then he prays to this unknown God who has created heaven and earth and has commanded the people to seek him, "and perhaps grope for him and find him – though indeed he is not far from each one of us. For 'in him we live and move and have our being'; as even some of your own poets have said, 'For we too are his offspring.'" (Acts 17:27f)

Through his Ascension Christ has lifted us into God. Now we can truly say of ourselves that we move in God and that we live and are in God. Paul here adopts the teachings of the Stoics and Epicureans, who were actively publicising their philosophies in Athens at the time. He does not interpret this statement in a pantheistic sense, but rather in the light of the Resurrection of Jesus. Because God has woken Jesus from the dead and lifted him into heaven, we live in heaven here on earth, we are already in God. Paul quotes from his fellow Sicilian, the poet Aratus. The quote is from the didactic poem 'Phaenomena', which Aratus composed around 270 BC: "We are of God's kind". In these words the dignity of the person, such as it manifested itself in the ascension of Christ, was expressed 300 years before Jesus was active. Paul here connects with the wisdom of the Greeks, in order to proclaim to them a message which fulfils the longing of their philosophers. Interpreters disagree about whether we are of God's kind by nature, or whether we become thus only through Christ. Luke leaves this question open. For him the decisive point is that the Greeks' intuitions were fulfilled in Jesus Christ. On account of Jesus' Ascension we as Christians can truly say, "We are of God's kind". Everywhere we go, we are immersed in God, wrapped in his healing and loving presence. In God we breathe, in God we weep, in God we rejoice, in God we mourn. We possess true life only if we are in God. Luke here uses the word 'zomen', which refers to a more essential life. Only life in God is true life. The Greek philosophers taught that God is true being. Our being has always taken part in the eternal being of God. Without God we fall into nothingness. Luke has shown in Paul's speech on the Areopagus that the fact of the Resurrection and Ascension of Jesus decisively influences our image of God and our image of the human person. God and humanity are one: never God without humanity, never humanity without God. This is probably the most beautiful statement ever made regarding the relationship between God and humanity. Not only are we related to God, but in him we live, move and are; because we are of God's kind, because our hearts have a divine core, because our relationship to him is an integral part of our being, we are created in his image and likeness.

Go through the day with this thought in mind; then will you realise who you truly are. Your life will acquire a new flavour. You will experience yourself differently. Imagine that you are in God at every moment and in him you move. When you walk, you go in God. When you breathe, you breathe in God. When you make a gesture, you make it not only before God, but in God. Believe that this idea is not just imagination, but reality, and it will lead you into the mystery of your life and show you your true dignity.

1. In the context of prayer, a position in which a person while standing extends their arms and holds them up.

Waiting for the Spirit

SEVENTH WEEK OF EASTER

Come, Holy Spirit

(Acts 1:12-14)

From the Ascension of Christ to Pentecost the Church holds a novena to the Holy Spirit. In doing so, it imitates the Apostles who returned to Jerusalem after Jesus' ascension and waited in the upper room in prayer, "together with certain women, including Mary the mother of Jesus, as well as his brothers" (Acts 1:14). They waited in prayer for the fulfilment of the promise which Jesus had given them before he ascended into heaven. "But you will receive power when the Holy Spirit has come upon you" (Acts 1:8). In the Pentecostal novena we longingly wait for the Holy Spirit to come down on us, too, on the Church whose existence is meaningless without the Holy Spirit, on everybody in person – so that all that is dried up and withered within us may become alive again. The Romans already had prayers lasting for nine days; and since the twelfth century novenas have become popular in Christian piety. The word 'nine' is similar to the word 'new' in many languages (e.g. Latin 'novem' and 'novis'). The number nine symbolises transformation. It prepares a new 'gestalt', a new way of being, just as the child spends nine months in its mother's womb before it is born. The original Christian novena is the Pentecostal novena prayed by the Apostles, with Mary and the women who accompanied Jesus. In the Pentecostal novena we pray for the renewal of the Church and for our own personal rebirth.

In evening vespers during the Pentecostal novena the hymn 'Veni creator spiritus' is sung, which was composed by the Benedictine monk Rabanus Maurus around 809. The words of Rabanus Maurus penned originally in Latin almost 1200 years ago, express a longing we still feel today:

> Come, Holy Ghost, Creator, come
> From thy bright heavenly throne,
> Come, take possession of our souls,
> And make them all thy own.

May the Spirit draw out of us once more that life which has lost its strength in the toils of everyday living. Many today long to feel alive, to live life authentically; it seems to them that the life they lead has little in common with true life. God has created the world through the Spirit: may it create us anew. We breathe in physically all the time – this act of breathing should help us to understand how God continually renews us through the breath of his Spirit.

> Thou who art called the Paraclete,
> Best gift of God above,
> The living spring, the living fire,
> Sweet unction and true love.

The Holy Spirit is our helper and consoler, a gift of the Father; a living spring, a fire, a light, love and unction ('fons vivus, ignis, caritas et spiritalis unctio'). The Holy Spirit is the spring of life. We are able to draw from this spring without ever exhausting it, because it is divine. Many today feel dried up, spent, burnt out, because they are constantly called upon to give. In the Pentecostal novena we plead that the spring of the Holy Spirit may well up in us again and refresh and strengthen us. The Holy Spirit is also fire and light, it warms us and enlightens us. And it is unction, which heals our wounds and calls each one of us to the task we have been assigned.

I do not want to look at all the stanzas of this memorable hymn, but I cannot pass over the fourth stanza. It reads:

> O guide our minds with thy blest light,
> With love our hearts inflame;
> And with thy strength which ne'er decays,
> Confirm our mortal frame.

The original Latin in its literal sense requests that the Holy Spirit provide a light for our senses ('accende lumen sensibus'). The Holy Spirit is not something that has to do purely with the spiritual and mental. It seeks, rather, to inflame our senses, brightening them so that we are able to perceive God in this world through them. When we are awake in our senses then our life becomes truly as God intended it. We will be truly present in this world. Our senses put us in touch with reality. When we chant this plea, we can feel how dull our senses often are, how we do not feel much of what is around us, because we are somewhere else with our thoughts, not in our senses. When the senses are shaken up and illuminated by the Holy Spirit, they become the actual vehicle through which we experience God. We do not experience God with our head, but with our senses, by hearing God's voice amid the many voices and by seeing the invisible in the visible.

The Holy Spirit is at the same time the love that is poured out into our hearts. Ultimately, each one of us longs to love and to be loved. The Holy Spirit not only enables us to love, it is also the love of the Father that pours into our hearts. In the Holy Spirit we feel ourselves loved by God fully and wholly. In the Holy Spirit the divine love flows through our heart and our body. The last plea of this stanza concerns our body and its weaknesses: may the Holy Spirit permeate our body, in particular, with new strength. The Holy Spirit seeks always to incarnate itself, and desires to become fixed in our flesh and fill it with divine strength.

In the days of the Pentecostal novena, join the ranks of the men and women who are waiting together in the upper room for the coming of the Holy Spirit. In this germ-cell, formed by the praying disciples of Jesus, male and female, the new has begun to germinate – and in a short while it will conquer the whole world. The upper room is like a mother's womb from which the Church is born. And from this womb you are born as a new person. Meditate on Rabanus Maurus' hymn of 1200 years ago, and let the images work themselves deep inside you! Then, perhaps, you will feel the spring of the Holy Spirit beginning to well up in you again and the flame of his love kindling anew in you.

• MONDAY •

The Spirit as the rush of a mighty wind

(Acts 2:2)

In his narrative of the Pentecostal event, Luke describes the Holy Spirit using a variety of images. Probably the most impressive image is that of the rush of a mighty wind. The Disciples were all in the same place, "and suddenly from heaven there came a sound like the rush of a mighty wind, and it filled the entire house where they were sitting" (Acts 2:2). The Disciples heard a sound like that of a mighty wind approaching. The Holy Spirit manifests itself audibly and perceptibly. We hear the roaring of the wind with our ears, but we can also feel the rush of the wind on our skin. It drives through us, makes us move, shakes us through. From the very beginning the Bible has described the Spirit of God as air, breath and mighty wind. The breath of God hovered above the waters at creation. For me the image of wind is important for our experience of the Holy Spirit. Many think that the Holy Spirit is something intangible, abstract. This is why so many struggle with it. They try to believe in it, but it does not mean anything to them. But if I stand in the wind and feel with all my senses how it caresses my skin, my perception of the Holy Spirit will change. The Holy Spirit can caress me with a gentle breeze; in a violent storm it blows through me, blowing all the dust out of me. Or it can make me move and drive me forward, because I cannot resist the mighty wind. The Holy

Spirit can be felt in my breath, too: I breathe in not only the air, but also God's holy and healing Spirit. And through this Spirit I breathe in his love, which permeates me.

Elijah had to learn that rather than being in the storm, God was in the sound of a gentle breeze. At Pentecost the Holy Spirit comes as the rush of a mighty wind. We must not try to limit the way in which the Spirit of God acts: it can come to us very quietly, so that we only perceive it in silence; but it can also sweep us along into a state of stormy enthusiasm, so that we shed all inhibitions and simply have to tell others what we have experienced. On Pentecost Day the Disciples were gathered together and formed the germ-cell of the Church. It is not just a question of our individual experience of God, therefore, but of the movement which the Holy Spirit brings into the Church. Pope John XXIII caught the spirit of Pentecost when he called before the start of the Council on all Christians to open their windows wide, that the Holy Spirit might bring new life into the Church and blow out all the stuffiness, and that a fresh wind might blow in the parishes. Each Pentecost we ask God to send us his Holy Spirit, that the Church might not lose heart, might not go round in circles and lick its wounds, but that it might have the courage to step out of itself and be able to awaken storms of enthusiasm in the people. Think about the different qualities the wind possesses: at times it caresses you tenderly, it moves the grass to and fro; but it can also throw trees down, lash across the earth with an irresistible force. If you listen to the wind when you are in the forest, you can sometimes sense a mysterious atmosphere and thus get some intuition of the mystery of the Holy Spirit. Imagine that in the wind the Holy Spirit himself breathes around you and penetrates inside you. Be wholly in your breath and through your senses enter fully into your breath: see how in your breath God's holy and loving Spirit flows into you and penetrates and transforms everything within you. If you do that, the Holy Spirit will no longer seem abstract and unconnected to the world. You will sense it in the same way as you sense the wind, which you also cannot see, but which you recognise by its actions, by the rustling it creates, by the swaying of the grass, by the dust that is carried aloft. Trust that the Holy Spirit in you has the same strength as the wind, that it can move you to new life.

• TUESDAY •

The Holy Spirit as fire

(Acts 2:3)

The second image which Luke uses to describe the Pentecostal mystery is that of fire: "Divided tongues, as of fire, appeared among them, and a tongue rested on each of them." (Acts 2:3) Whereas the storm is primarily audible, the tongues of fire are primarily visible. In this guise the Holy Spirit can be seen. This is the mystery of Pentecost: that which is invisible becomes visible. The image of the tongues of fire is known in rabbinic literature: the word of God comes down on individuals in tongues of fire. Through this use of the image of the divided flames Luke tells us that every single person is filled with the Holy Spirit, that every person is inflamed by the Spirit of God.

Fire is considered holy in many cultures. While water springs forth from the earth, fire comes from heaven. Fire is something divine. For this very reason many cultures have fire gods. Fire purifies and renews. That which is incomplete, it makes pure. Gold is purified in fire, all the dross is burnt out, leaving only the gold itself. The Holy Spirit wants to burn away everything which hinders the life within us. There is much obscurity within us, and spirits of obscurity such as bitterness, discontent, hurts, insults. All these spirits of obscurity hinder us from living. We cannot make clear decisions, they become clouded over by our annoyance, our jealousy, our feelings of inferiority. In our confusion, we long for the fire of the Holy Spirit, which will burn out all that is clouded and discoloured, so that we may be able to decide with a clear and pure heart. Fire is a preparation for rebirth on a higher level. When what is old in us is burnt out, new life is able to spring forth.

Fire is also an image of being alive. People are described as having flashing eyes. They emanate something; sparks seem to leap from them to others. They radiate life, joy, awakeness. It is impossible not to feel the effect they exert. But the fire that burns in the eyes of some does not warm: it flares and makes us wince. We feel somehow that there is something evil and incalculable in these people.

When we ask for the fire of the Holy Spirit, we ask for the fire which awakens life, which rekindles within us the flame that had burnt low. Many today feel empty and burnt out. The burn-out syndrome is particularly widespread among people in the caring professions who overtax themselves for the sake of others. Only those who burn, can burn out. But these people have forgotten to watch over their inner fire – as Henri Nouwen understands the task of the spiritual life. They keep the door of their oven constantly open, and so all they are left with is ashes. Nothing emanates from them any more. They are resigned and disappointed, without strength and without a spark. The message of Pentecost is that in the depth of our heart there is not just ashes, but glowing embers from which body and soul can be inflamed anew. Not for nothing are red liturgical garments worn at Pentecost, in order to remind us of this inner flame. We celebrate Pentecost so that the glowing embers within us may burst into flame anew, a flame which warms others and gives them joy, which helps them discover their own aliveness.

In my youth we liked to sit around a campfire and sing songs together. There is something fascinating about gazing into the fire together. Fire binds us together. The community gathers around the fire. Thus we ask in the Pentecostal novena that the fire may not just come down on the individual person, but that the fire of the Holy Spirit may become the centre around which people gather, that the Church may become a place where we sit around the fire together, to sing the songs of our longing, songs which lift our heart to God.

What is your experience of fire? What do you associate with fire? What thoughts does it trigger in you? Trust that the fire of the Holy Spirit burns in you, the fire of love, the fire of aliveness, imagination and strength! Guard this fire in you, so that it may not go out! The Germanic tribes of the past considered it a duty to watch over the hearth fire; anyone who let it go out, was punished severely. Let the fire in your hearth burn, so that it may warm, purify and renew everything within you, that everything in you may be permeated by God's love! If you guard the fire within you, and provide it with fuel, then others will be able to warm themselves by it. Their eyes will light up, and new aliveness radiate from them.

• WEDNESDAY •

The Holy Spirit and the new language

(Acts 2:4-13)

The third image that Luke uses to describe the effect of the Holy Spirit is the image of language: "All of them were filled with the Holy Spirit and began to speak in other languages, as the Spirit gave them ability." (Acts 2:4) The image refers back to the confusion of languages as narrated by the Book of Genesis. In the beginning, "the whole earth had one language and the same words" (Gen 11:1). This gave the inhabitants of the earth great power. But this power made them proud and they wanted to build a tower that would reach into heaven. Therefore God decided, "Come, let us go down, and confuse their language there, so that they will not understand one another's speech." (Gen 11:7) When someone no longer understands what the other means, then it is not possible to work together. The reverse is true as well, however: when people speak the same language, they can accomplish great things together. This is something we experience today in many groups, parishes, businesses, political parties. When a common language is lost, communities fall apart, and although individuals might accomplish great things, it is always in isolation.

Pentecost is God's answer to the Babylonian confusion of languages. God wants people to speak the same language again, thereby enabling them to create something new and permanent. God gives humankind through the Holy Spirit a common language, so that together we can steward his creation responsibly, so that the many peoples and cultures can grow together to form a large family.

In his account of the happenings at Pentecost Luke uses two words for 'talking'. The first of these is the word 'lalein', which actually means 'to chatter', 'to chat', 'to talk in a familiar way with each other'. The Disciples speak in different languages with great naturalness, in a familiar tone, as it were. And everyone can understand them. This astonishes the people from the different nations, and they ask: "Are not all these who are speaking Galileans? And how is it that we hear, each of us, in our own native language?" (Acts 2:7f) The other word is 'apophtheggesthai', which means, 'to talk enthusiastically, ecstatically'. The Disciples don't just talk about anything, but they proclaim "God's deeds of power" (Acts 2:11). The people allow themselves to be infected by the enthusiasm of the Disciples: "All were amazed and perplexed" (Acts 2:12).

The Holy Spirit enables us to speak a new language, a language understood by all, and to speak with an enthusiasm which infects and inflames others. In the Church of today we suffer from our speechlessness. In the first place, we are hardly able to talk to each other. We talk at cross-purposes, as did the people in Babylonia. The representatives of the various tendencies within the Church are no longer able to communicate with each other. In the second place, our language has become empty. We are no longer able to get through to people. They feel that the language of the Church has become an insider's language, which has ceased to enthuse them and sweep them away. A journalist expressed the irrelevance of the Church's language as follows: "God is not dead. It's just that he fell asleep during 'Thought for the Day'". We are obviously unable to talk about God in the same way as the Disciples were at Pentecost. Our language does not touch the human heart. Many sermons, one feels, say something which is right, but they just go right past the people listening. And nothing moves in their hearts.

According to Luke, any language that connects people and moves their hearts must meet two conditions. As a first condition, we must learn to have the courage to talk 'in a familiar way'; we must learn, for example, to express ourselves in the same way as we would when we are with those close to us, sharing that which moves our hearts. Some hide behind their language: their do not speak from their heart; one does not sense what they actually want to say; they talk about something, not about themselves, and what they say does not come out of themselves. Others will only understand our language if it comes from the heart, if we say what we have experienced, what we are currently experiencing, or something we have some intuition about. Perhaps the things we try to express will still be a little unclear and we might not be able to do more than chat about them (lalein). But by having the courage to say what is inside us, the shapeless begins to take shape. Others then feel: 'You have expressed the very thing which I have felt for some time, something I wasn't able to put into words'. When our words cause this type of reaction, then the Holy Spirit has inspired us. The second condition is that we talk 'enthusiastically', that we allow ourselves to be torn out of pure objectivity, that we let our hearts be touched by the storm of the Spirit. Something of this strength of the Spirit has to flow in our speech, so that it is able to enthuse others. This does not mean that we should manipulate others. Some people are demagogues who twist their words, and by addressing peoples' unconscious needs they gain power over them through their words. The language that the Holy Spirit inspires in us has a healing and liberating effect on people. It puts people in touch with their deep longing and opens their hearts, so that God's love can stream into it. Luke describes two effects of the new language. The people step out of themselves, they lose their composure, they change, transform. The language causes something new to emerge inside of them. They enter into a different state. And they become puzzled and embarrassed. They lose some of their self-assurance. The words of the Apostles make them think and question. They say to each other: "What does this mean?" (Acts 2:12)

When you speak, how do you speak? Do you say what is in your heart? Or do you hide behind meaningless words? Can you enthuse others when you speak? Or do your words go straight over their heads?

Meditate on the Bible and make its language your own! The unusual language it contains seeks to make something move inside you. Allow yourself to be discomfited by the words of the Holy Scripture! Leave your old state, your secure position! What is it that the words of the Bible want to coax out of you? Do their currents want to sweep you along and deposit you on a new shore? Let the words fall into your heart, let them help you continue on your way along the path which leads to your true self, on your journey to God!

• THURSDAY •

The Holy Spirit as helper

(John 14-16)

In five passages in John's Gospel Jesus promises his Disciples to send the Holy Spirit to help them. The Greek word used, 'parakletos', can mean, 'the one called to come', 'the advocate, who speaks on a person's behalf at court and defends them'. But this helper also comforts and encourages. Jesus promises the Disciples a helper who will be with them forever (cf. Jn 14:16f). He calls the helper the Spirit of truth. His task is to teach them and remind them of everything that Jesus has told them (Jn 14:26). And the helper is to give witness on behalf of Jesus (Jn 15:26). The Holy Spirit will help the Disciples when they are brought before the courts. He will inspire them with the right words. As Jesus promised in Matthew's Gospel, it is "the Spirit of your Father speaking through you" (Mt 10:20). The Holy Spirit is not only an advocate, however, but also a prosecutor. He "will prove the world wrong about sin and righteousness and judgement" (Jn 16:8). The most important task of the helper is to initiate the Disciples into the whole truth (Jn 16:13). He will not tell the Disciples anything new, but open up the words of Jesus in their true meaning: "He will glorify me, because he will take what is mine and declare it to you." (Jn 16:14)

The communities to whom John dedicated his Gospel found this image to be of great value. It helped them to survive in the hostile atmosphere of Roman religious policy. But what meaning does this image have for us today? It is important for me to know that I am not alone in my faith. I do not stand alone against a world that has closed itself to the faith. Even when I myself am tempted to feel that being a monk, I am a relic of earlier times, I nevertheless remain convinced in my innermost being that the spiritual path is the true path to life. The Holy Spirit helps me on my path. Through him I gain certainty that my path is right. Participants in the courses I give sometimes tell me that they often feel lost in the world on account of their faith. The Church is mocked at their place of work. Christian ideas are ridiculed. They so often feel alone, feel like they are fighting a losing battle. If I can remember that the Holy Spirit is my helper, I will be able to trust what my heart tells me, in spite of all the questioning I face. In my heart the Holy Spirit speaks. The Holy Spirit is by my side. He stands by me. He backs me up. I can, and am allowed to, think differently from the people around me. I am allowed to speak and live differently. With the Holy Spirit at my back I feel myself to be authentic and free. The Holy Spirit wants to leads us into the full truth. He lifts the veil that covers everything. All too often we grope in the dark. We talk about reality, but ultimately we talk only about the ideas we ourselves have formed of reality. When the Holy Spirit lifts the veil, we are able to recognise the whole truth. We get the bigger picture. We now can see right to the bottom of things. Everything becomes suddenly clear. Only through the Holy Spirit can I understand the words of Jesus in a way that they affect my specific situation; only through the Spirit will they become words of life, words that lead me to life. Sometimes I stand before the words of the Bible and do not understand them. They remain alien to me, cumbersome, and all too often annoying. Then I pray to the Holy Spirit to interpret the words for me, so that they speak to me and I can see their relevance. And sometimes, not only will the meaning of the words become clear to me, but the words will become carriers of life and of love, they will lead me into the mystery of God.

Carry this image of the Holy Spirit as a helper with you through the day! Imagine that you are not left to rely on yourself alone when you must face conflict, when others ask you to account for something, when you are facing a difficult task, when your religious belief makes you feel isolated! The Holy Spirit stands by you. He stands next to you, looks at you and inspires you with the thoughts and words that help you along.

• FRIDAY •

The gifts of the Holy Spirit

(1 Corinthians 12:8-11)

In the First Letter to the Corinthians Paul talks about the different gifts of grace that are given to Christians by the same Spirit. These gifts are given to the individual so that they can serve others with them. Paul talks about charisms: gifts, abilities, characteristics which God gives to each human person. Heribert Mühlen defines a charism as something which "enables a person to life and service in the Church and the world, which flows from grace (*charis*) and which is especially assigned by the Holy Spirit in each case" (*LexSpir)*. We do not possess these gifts, but they are given to us as each situation requires. For Paul it is important that all gifts stream forth from the same Spirit of God: "To one is given through the Spirit the utterance of wisdom, and to another the utterance of knowledge according to the same Spirit, to another faith by the same Spirit, to another gifts of healing by the one Spirit, to another the working of miracles, to another prophecy, to another the discernment of spirits, to another various kinds of tongues, to another the interpretation of tongues. All these are activated by one and the same Spirit, who allots to each one individually just as the Spirit chooses." (1 Cor 12:8-11) Today, we run a great danger of directing our gaze exclusively to our hurts and limitations; we think that we must deal with our wounds and the obstructions within us before we can truly live. We certainly cannot ignore our injuries, but we must not become fixated on them either. Here the perspective that Paul invites us to share, is helpful and healing: look at the gifts that the Holy Spirit has given each of us. Every person has a particular gift. God has given each one of us abilities and potential that characterise us alone. Everyone can contribute something to the life of the community. Everyone is valuable in their own way. It is a question of recognising the gift that has been given me. Time and again I meet people who do not think themselves capable of anything. They think it unfair that others are more gifted. Someone is musical; someone else is always in good heath and cheerful, whereas I have to contend with my depression and feel worthless because others are better at everything. Instead of comparing themselves against others, such people should look at what God has in mind for them. In everyone there is something precious, distinctive, special, a unique gift. Looking at my own life story will help me discern my gift. The things I have experienced and suffered, constitute my gift. When I have been hurt much, then my gift is perhaps an ability to understand and accompany others better. When my human needs have not been met, then I am perhaps particularly gifted to take a spiritual path. When I feel my limitations painfully, then my gift is perhaps a mildness and loving kindness towards myself and others.

When I look at Paul's list, I am struck by the fact that the gift that is most highly esteemed by the Corinthians comes last. The Corinthians especially loved speaking in tongues. They understood this to be the divine language. But it is a language which cannot be understood. Paul criticises this striking phenomenon. For him the gifts which institute a relationship are more important. A person who helps someone gain an insight, is active in the Holy Spirit. A person who cures an illness, who soothes wounds, has a gift of the Holy Spirit. Above all these gifts, however, Paul places the blessed gift of love. Without love the greatest gifts remain useless and empty (1 Cor 13).

Church Tradition speaks of the seven gifts of the Holy Spirit. Following Isaiah 11:1-5, they are: the spirit of wisdom and of understanding, the spirit of counsel and of might, the spirit of knowledge and piety, and the spirit of the fear of the Lord. Seven is the number of transformation. The purpose of the Holy Spirit's seven gifts is to transform humankind into the true image of ourselves, as God intended. The Pentecostal sequence ascribes to the seven gifts the ability to convey the reward of virtue ('virtutis meritum'), ultimate salvation ('salutis exitum') and eternal joy ('perenne gaudium'). We cannot simply call the seven gifts of the Holy Spirit down upon ourselves. They are a gift. But we should nevertheless earnestly desire them: while Paul talks about the fact that these gifts are God-given, he nevertheless calls on us to "strive for the greater gifts" (1 Cor 12:31). When we let these seven gifts act within us, our life will blossom, it will become healed and whole and filled with a joy that endures even beyond death.

What gifts has God given to you? And which among the many gifts characterises you most? Each gift is also a task. Its presence is designed to lead you to life, while it also enables you to build others up, to be of use to others, as Paul says. When you have found out your gifts, then live them, put them to use for yourself and for other people! In your gift, develop your uniqueness freely and serve others! Be sensitive to where people today have a particular need of you and your gifts! Believe that the Holy Spirit can give you, at the critical moment, the gift through which you will restore people, help them back onto their feet and fill them with new life!

• SATURDAY •

The miracle of Pentecost in the community

(Acts 4:23-31)

In the Acts of the Apostles Luke describes a number of scenes in which the miracle of Pentecost is repeated in the community. Pentecost is a unique event, but it is not unrepeatable, it can happen each time the community gathers around Jesus Christ and prays together with its Risen Lord to the Father. This we can see in the scene reported in Acts 4:23-31. After being released by the High Priests, Peter and John return to their communities and report everything to them. The community responds by raising their voices to God 'in unison' and praying. They praise God's great deeds, as they had been revealed in Jesus Christ, and conclude with the following plea: "And now, Lord, look at their threats, and grant to your servants to speak your word with all boldness, while you stretch out your hand to heal, and signs and wonders are performed through the name of your holy servant Jesus." (Acts 4:29f) Faced by many threats, the community pleads above all for 'parresia', the freedom to say what the Spirit inspires. To believe in the Holy Spirit means to proclaim the words which come from God in freedom, without fear of man. When wonders and miracles never cease, then we know the Holy Spirit is present.

Following the community's prayer God performs the miracle of Pentecost: "When they had prayed, the place in which they were gathered together was shaken; and they were all filled with the Holy Spirit and spoke the word of God with boldness." (Acts 4:31) As at Pentecost, the place starts shaking. Among the Greeks, shaking was a sign of prayer being answered. Luke here obviously adopts a Hellenistic motif in order to translate the Christian message into terms that the Greeks would find more understandable and appealing. Luke describes the Holy Spirit's effect with the Greek word 'saleuo', meaning 'move', 'swing', 'shake', 'tremble', 'sway', 'waver'. The Holy Spirit generates movement within the community. Hearts become one, they move together. They are shaken and made to tremble. The entire person is moved from the inside. From this movement there comes strength. This strength is clear for all to see, since now they all proclaim the word of God openly, they shed their fear of man and say what God inspires them to say without misgivings.

After the Pentecostal event in the second chapter and the Pentecostal experience in the fourth chapter Luke describes the life of the community. For him the Holy Spirit is the one who forms the Church, who makes it possible for people to live together in a new way. It is a miracle that people with differing characters and from many different backgrounds are able to become one: "Now the whole group of those who believed were of one heart and soul, and no one claimed private ownership of any possessions, but everything they owned was held in common. With great power the apostles gave their testimony to the Resurrection of the Lord Jesus, and great grace was upon them all." (Acts 4:32f) A sign of true community is the willingness to share goods. From community comes great strength. It is the strength of the Spirit, the Spirit which enabled Jesus to accomplish his great deeds. Luke, in describing the miracle of Pentecost and the new way of living together that it created in the community, aims to encourage and lift us up as well. All we have to do is to keep praying with one voice and be prepared to engage with each other and to share our life together. If we were to do this, then the Church today would become a centre of great strength, a place filled with an atmosphere of freedom and openness; then wonders would never cease: the discouraged would be raised up, the sick, healed and those without hope, would start hoping again.

You might feel that today's Church lacks such miracles of Pentecost. In many services there is no sense that the congregation moves in unison. The Church does not appear to be a refuge of freedom and of encouragement. But in the very midst of a Church which has in many places become tired you can, time and again, discover new places where the Spirit causes new life to spring up again. In such places the earth moves, wonders never cease. Trust in the Holy Spirit: he can make your community or parish move; there, too, people can find healing for their wounds, and inner freedom! Perhaps today the Holy Spirit would like to bring together, liberate and heal people through you, and you especially.

Pentecost

THE FIFTIETH DAY

THE FIFTIETH DAY

The Holy Spirit and the fulfilment of the human person

The word Pentecost is derived from the Greek 'pentekoste', meaning 'fifty'. It is the fiftieth day after Easter. Pentecost is the fulfilment of Easter. Both feasts have their origin in nature festivals celebrated in Palestine. Easter is the spring festival, Pentecost marks the beginning of the wheat harvest. The Jewish people used events from its history of salvation to interpret both festivals. So Easter became the remembrance of the Exodus from Egypt, Pentecost the remembrance of the handing over of the commandments on Sinai. For us Christians Easter is the feast of the Resurrection of Jesus and Pentecost the feast of the sending of the Spirit. Every feast is also always a feast of human self-becoming. At Pentecost we celebrate the fulfilment of the incarnation. In order to understand what Pentecost has to do with the process of our becoming whole, it might help to have a closer look at the origins of this feast.

To start with there is the number fifty. At fifty, a person is on the threshold of old age. In Rome people were exempt from military service once they turned 50. Augustine interpreted the number 50 symbolically: "This fiftieth day, however, has another mysterious meaning. Seven times seven is forty-nine, and when we return to the beginning and add an eighth day, which is also the first, the figure of 50 is completed. These fifty days after the

Resurrection of the Lord are celebrated no longer as a symbol of hardship, but as a symbol of peace and joy." (Betz) Fifty is thus an image of peace and joy. At 50, thought Pope Gregory the Great, a person becomes wise, becomes a person of the Spirit. He derived this interpretation from the instruction of Moses, which obliged the Levites from 25 years of age to serve at the tent of the Revelation. Their service ended at 50, when the Levites became the protectors of holy vessels. For Pope Gregory this Scripture passage provided an image of the task of direction which had been entrusted to Benedict at the age of 50 (cf. Lev 8:24ff). Tauler refers to Gregory's interpretation when he says that the human person goes through a spiritual crisis in the middle of life, aged 40. Until then, their image of God is much too clouded by projection. In the years between 40 and 50, however, the Holy Spirit transforms the person's relationship with God and enables them to understand and experience him (or her). At the age of 50, finally, we become people of the Spirit, a source of blessing for others, able to initiate them into the wisdom and experience of God.

In Israel the 50th year was considered a jubilee year: "you shall not sow, or reap the aftergrowth, or harvest the unpruned vines. For it is a jubilee; it shall be holy to you: you shall eat only what the field itself produces." (Lev 25:11f) At the same time all debts were to be cancelled and all slaves were to be set free again. This is a beautiful image of the incarnation. The 50th year is supposed to be a year of reflection, a Sabbath year during which we stop to reflect on what has been unjust in our lives, what did not grow in accordance with our own being and the will of God. We are called to remit all sins, that is, we are supposed to settle all our differences with others, clarify our relationships; but it is also a time to reconcile ourselves with ourselves and with our lives. And we are called to set our slaves free. We are asked to liberate all that we have kept in slavery, all that we have suppressed, so that it can truly live. We are called to cease to live as slaves ourselves – living as wage-slaves, proving our value by how well we perform – but instead live as a free son, free daughter of God.

The Pentecostal feast reverberates with all these ideas. When the Holy Spirit comes upon us, then the symbolic number 50 comes to fulfilment in us, and then we reach our true being, calm and joyful, and are enabled to become the guardian of holy vessels, that is, to direct and accompany others. The 50 days between Easter and Pentecost are meant to initiate us into the incarnation. The Easter Gospels and Easter stories, the narrative of the Ascension of Christ and the sending of the Spirit at Pentecost describe the path of human self-becoming – the path of the rising from the tomb, of the Resurrection amid our daily lives, of the descent into our own humanity, towards heaven, which is in us. It is the path which leads us from the Risen One who accompanies us to the inner master who talks within us. Our self-becoming includes both the waiting for, and the sending of, the Spirit which we celebrate at Pentecost. When the Spirit comes, we come to ourselves, our capabilities and our potentialities are roused, everything in us becomes transformed. The blossom opens and our lives bloom. Pentecost is the feast of being alive. When the Spirit of God, which hovered over the creation at the beginning, penetrates us, we are newly created, we get in touch with our own origins, we grow into the true image of ourselves, as God intended.

Pentecost does not just refer to the growth and the self-becoming of the person, but also to that of the Church. Pentecost is the birth of the Church. When the Holy Spirit descends upon the people, he brings them together, he enables them to form a community which is open for all those who seek and who question. A community is created, which is able to transcend its own narrow confines and becomes the leaven for the world. A person can complete their own self-becoming only if they engage with the community and tackle with it the task which God has given us all: to make this world more human, to shape this world according to God's will and to leave the mark of God's Spirit upon it. The Church is the community of those who together give witness to the Resurrection of Jesus. Wherever those without hope are to be found, where the darkness of death seems to conquer life, the Church should witness to the victory of life over death, to the victory of love over hatred, to the possibility of Resurrection amid death.

Pentecostal rites

Even though Pentecost is full of meaning for the path of our own incarnation and the new togetherness we experience, less and less people know how to celebrate it. Perhaps this is also because the

Church has not developed any specific rites for Pentecost. Christmas and Easter are deeply imprinted on peoples' souls because of the impressive rituals that are celebrated during Midnight Mass on Christmas Eve and during the Easter Vigil. For many, the Pentecostal service seems like any other. For this reason, it might be helpful to look out for old Pentecostal rites and to adapt them to our own time, so that the mystery of the feast can imprint itself more deeply onto the human soul.

The liturgy at Pentecost is characterised by red liturgical garments, symbolic of the ardour which the Holy Spirit wants to enkindle in us. Pentecost is the time when we are invited to get in touch with the inner fire. In some parts of Germany, for example, there is the Pentecostal ride, or the festive driving of the cattle to Alpine pastures. Both customs show that at Pentecost the people are drawn to the outdoors, that the idea of beauty of the creation is included in the liturgical celebration of this feast. Walking together and marvelling at nature in bloom would be a very good Pentecostal rite. Pentecostal rites could involve the water. The Holy Spirit is the spring that wells up inside us. The spring has always been an archetypal symbol of that renewal of life which God's Spirit within us makes possible. It would be fitting, then, at Pentecost to go looking for springs and to note how they well up incessantly: an image of the source that wells up within us, of the spring within us which is inexhaustible because it is divine. Or we could sit down by a brook or river and simply watch the water flowing. So life begins to flow again when the Holy Spirit makes that which is inflexible and frozen in us, and that which is dried up and withered, flowing and fertile again.

Through the Holy Spirit the earth was created. The Holy Spirit permeates the entire creation. When we walk through nature we can imagine that the spirit which pours forth from each tree and each flower, flows within us as well; that the power of life, which we encounter everywhere, particularly at Pentecost, is in us too. Or we could turn into the wind and feel it on our faces and bodies. So the Holy Spirit caresses us tenderly or blows through us and blows all the cobwebs out of us. Or we might stand in the sun and feel the warmth of divine love, which flows into us through the Holy Spirit, how it penetrates our whole body. And so we will feel truly touched by God's love that is poured out in our hearts in the Holy Spirit, as Paul writes in his Letter to the Romans (Rom 5:5).

Another good Pentecostal rite would be to prepare bits of paper for the Pentecostal service, each of which has a gift of the Holy Spirit written on it. After communion each participant in the service could take one of the pieces, and then try to live the gift that they have drawn. We do not have to limit ourselves to the seven gifts of the Holy Spirit or to the charisms that Paul lists in the First Letter to the Corinthians. All the abilities which God gives us are gifts of the Spirit: there is the gift of reconciliation, of optimism, of healing, of direction, of peace, of attentiveness, of trust, of openness, of consolation, of understanding, of cleverness. Once during a Pentecostal course we did this, and let the participants draw a card with one of the gifts of the Spirit: we sensed how much this triggered in them.

Many thought about why they had drawn their particular card. Some did not think they had the abilities for their gift. Some were frightened by their gift. But a gift is not a demand. A man who had drawn the gift of healing, wondered what to make of it. It does not mean that he should now think that he can heal all wounds. Rather, the gift enabled him to become sensitive to the fact that sometimes a healing effect emanates from us, that we are able to encourage others by a word, or that we are able to soothe many a wound through our humour. The aim of this gift was to sharpen awareness of the fact that people are healed through us. Each of us has more potential than we often think possible. The gift that we choose is never at random. It is always a challenge to explore more consciously the potential for the said gift that we actually possess already. A woman who had drawn the gift of leadership, was startled. She did not know how she might make use of it. But after a short discussion she suddenly felt that she would like to try and take the initiative in some situations and to tackle a problem within her family, which she had thought could not be resolved. Drawing a Pentecostal gift awakens new abilities in us. Through this rite we can make that which we celebrate at Pentecost become real in our own lives.

Conclusion

We have walked the fifty days from Easter to Pentecost. We have meditated on the Easter Gospels and on some stories from the Acts of the Apostles. I hope that on the path of the Resurrection you have experienced the new life of the Resurrection and that you have begun to touch your God-given potential and the joy which always comes when we accomplish something, when life blossoms within us. Each season of the Church's year is an initiation into the process of becoming more fully what we truly are. Advent and Christmastide are concerned with the new start which we celebrate in the birth of Christ. Lent is concerned with initiating us into inner freedom and reconciling us with the suffering which forms an integral part of our lives. Eastertide helps us to unfold the new life which was opened up in the Resurrection of Jesus and which finds its fulfilment in the sending of the Spirit at Easter. In Eastertide we are invited to get in touch with the joy which lies waiting at the bottom of our hearts, but which all too often is overshadowed by painful experiences or by our dissatisfaction. Joy is a source of life, which heals our wounds and gives us pleasure in living. Without a source of joy our life becomes stale.

Paradoxically, the unfolding of new life has been very much neglected in spiritual writings. It therefore seems important to me to follow the path of the Resurrection consciously, as a path into ever-greater aliveness, freedom, joy and love. Those who follow the path of the Resurrection consciously, experience the centre of Christian faith, the mystery of the death and Resurrection of Jesus, of the Ascension of Christ and the sending of the Spirit. At the same time, they are initiated into the mystery of human self-becoming. The path of the incarnation necessarily involves, time after time, getting up, falling down, being buried, getting back on our feet, going away, taking leave; it involves the heaven that is above us, the experience of the inner master and the Holy Spirit, who is poured out in us and who brings the life within us to bloom, causing our abilities and our potential to unfold.

In the Resurrection stories we encounter people who react differently to the experience of Resurrection. They doubt, resist the challenge to get up again, close themselves off to the Spirit who wants to transform them. But many are finally overwhelmed by the power of the Resurrection and by the aliveness of the Holy Spirit. We see much of ourselves in these people. These companions on the way help us to see that we through our doubts and fears will find the path to Resurrection and fulfilment; that Easter and Pentecost can happen in our own daily lives, transforming them. My wish for you is this: May the path of the Resurrection lead you to the fullness of life which Christ has promised you and which the Church celebrates in Eastertide, that you may be gripped by the joy of Easter and that you may experience this joy not just in the time between Easter and Pentecost, but throughout the year – especially on Sundays, when we commemorate the Resurrection of Jesus in a very special way.

Bibliography

Prayers and Meditations of St Anselm, Ward, Benedicta (trans.), Penguin Books, 1973

Betz, Otto, *Das Geheimnis der Zahlen*, Stuttgart, 1989

Grundmann, Walter, *Das Evangelium nach Lukas*, Berlin, 1966

Grundmann, Walter, *Das Evangelium nach Matthäus*, Berlin, 1968

Jacobus de Voragine, *The Golden Legend or Lives of the Saints*, Caxton, William (trans.), Volume Four, Temple Classics, 1931

Mühlen, Heribert, 'Charisma', in: *LexSpir*, pp. 183-187

Pesch, Rudolf, *Die Apostelgeschichte*, Zurich, 1986

Pontikos, Evagrios, *On Prayer*, in: *The Philokalia*, Palmer, G.E.H., Sherrard, P., and Ware, K. (trans. and ed.), Faber and Faber, 1984

Rahner, Karl, *Kleines Kirchenjahr*, Munich, 1953

Hymns Old and New (ed.) Kevin Mayhew et al, Kevin Mayhew Limited, 1989

Where freely translated, references have been quoted with the bibliographical information of the original German source.